OUT ON A LIMB

A Single Father's Guide to his Family's Lore of the Jungle

by

Simon Turner

Published in Australia in 2014
by Out On A Limb Publications
PO Box 1150 Brighton QLD 4017
www.outonalimb.com.au

National Library of Australia
Cataloguing-in-Publication data:

Turner, Simon, 1972 - author.

Out on a limb : a single father's guide to his family's lore
of the jungle / Simon Turner.

9780992406509 (paperback)

Family law--Australia--Popular works.
Custody of children--Australia--Popular works.
Family mediation--Australia--Popular works.
Support (Domestic relations)--Australia--Popular works.
Divorce--Law and legislation--Australia--Popular works.
Single fathers--Australia--Popular works.

346.94015

Illustrations: Simon Turner
Design and layout: James Alley, Metagraphics.
www.metagraphics.com.au

Printed in Australia.

Dedication

There are two men named Damien in my life
One is my brother
The other is my barrister
I owe a lot to both

"Out on a Limb" **is a much needed, practical, down-to-earth, easy read for any bloke battling to avoid a war and remain a father to his children. This book proves that strength is a virtue not a weapon, well done Simon."**

- Ian (Watto) Watson,
(Founder of *"Shed Happens"* and author of *"Every Bloke's a Champion... Even You!")*

'Straight forward honest advice that could have saved me eight years of pain and heartache, not to mention a few dollars."

- John Anderson,
(Radio Surveyor)

www.outonalimb.com.au

FINISH WHAT YOU START

Preface

Out on a Limb is a book that is not backward in coming forward, and nor can it afford to be. In the lives of modern Australian men many things are placed in the 'too-hard basket', and gaining the care of their kids after a divorce or separation is one of them. In all honesty, I wish a book like this one had existed before I embarked on my all too painful and costly journey to ensure I had the opportunity to care and father my son. So one evening about a year after my battle had ended, and for no particular reason, I began writing down what had been learned about my family's lore of the jungle.

This book is not an account of all that happened to me; in fact there are no specific references to the particulars of my story. What this book contains are simple and practical suggestions drawn from a chanced but valued conversation. It is not legal advice, nor is it gospel but what you will find beyond this ramble are many answers to a multitude of questions you may have. For when you make your own journey through this jungle to find 'what's best for your kids' you'll discover all you need is some guidance, a lot of patience and a bit of help to reach an agreement.

Contents

THE LORE OF THE JUNGLE

1 The Three Golden Rules

Some say, in the beginning God (whether you believe in this idea or not) created man and woman. For argument's sake, let's call them Tarzan and Jane. But the truth is God can't be blamed for separation and divorce. That's the work of Jane and Tarzan. Though marriages are created with the best intentions, breaking up can be ugly, bitter and sometimes spiteful. Whatever we start in life will eventually come to an end, it seems, and by the end of the 20th century too many romances that grew into relationships and blossomed into marriage ended in separation and divorce.

The writer Mark Twain said, 'write what you know'. *Out on a Limb* doesn't draw solely on my experiences, but is reminiscent of observations and lessons I learned during my time in the jungle of family lore. In my career before becoming a full-time dad, I had the privilege of knowing some rather distinguished people, including professionals from across society. Often clients would offer me insights into life, but probably the most considered counsel came from judges. One judge's advice on learning of my 'predicament' radically changed my understanding and, ultimately, my situation. It offered me a way forward and out of the jungle that was encroaching and consuming every part of my life.

What he told me is not carved in stone or written in any book, but it was clear, straightforward and to the point. The judge looked me in the eye and said: 'There are three rules you need to understand. Rule number 1: *You both think you're right.* Rule number 2: *Show me you have the time.* Rule number 3: *Show me you have the place.*'

This advice didn't require an answer but some thought, and afterwards a fair bit of gratitude. I believe this simple explanation of incredibly complex matters of the heart and family can help any Tarzan work it out with his Jane to find a way out of the jungle.

Golden rule 1: 'You both think you're right.'

At first you may be a bit taken aback by this statement, but that just shows how true it is. The longer you search for a comeback to this statement, or try to justify your point of view, the longer it's going to take you to understand the simple truth of it. How long this takes is just a measure of your stubbornness. So take a deep breath, and take some solace in knowing that sometimes being or thinking you are right in this situation, is not the most important thing to be.

To some, the judge's point might appear to be obvious, yet 'that's why most (Tarzans and Janes) end up in court — because neither party is prepared to give'. Your case may be very different from the one the judge has just heard, but your reason for being in court is the same. At the heart of rule number 1 is the root of your whole dilemma. It doesn't matter which parent is 'right'. The only thing that matters is that you need to be able to agree on what's best for your kids. If you can take this advice on board, and are able to work it out with Jane without a mediator's or judge's assistance, you will undoubtedly save a lot of time, pain and money, not to mention your sanity. Plus your kids will be better off sooner rather than much later.

Golden rule 2: 'Show me you have the time.'

At first this rule too sounds simple enough, but after you begin to look seriously at your lifestyle and calendar, you may be in for a surprise. Having the time for your kids is not simply about your work commitments. It's also about things like where you now spend your time outside work, and who you spend it with. If you're at the pub drinking with your mates most afternoons, then enough said. Put simply, the pub is no place for a child.

Having time for the kids is not only about making yourself available on the weekend. It's about how much time you as a parent are willing and able to put into your children's lives and even more importantly how you think they should spend their time. It also extends to who you think they should spend time with including people like your family and relations. Remember, they're part of your children's family too. This information is very important to the judge. After all, judges aren't mind readers; they can only go by what's presented before them.

Golden rule 3: 'Show me you have the place.'

Again this sounds simple enough, but if you're still at the pub drinking with your mates, well, rule 2 will have quickly blurred into rule 3. This one has more to do with the children's environment, which includes the places they are familiar with and visit, where they spend their time, feel safe and, of course, where they live. It's more than just having a spare bedroom and a dog for the kids to play with. As any real-estate agent will tell you, it's about location, location, location — and this includes proximity. How close your new place is to Jane's, to childcare, to kindergarten and/or to school is very important. The further away you are in the jungle, the harder a shared care arrangement will be to manage. That's not to say that it can't be done, but if you move to the other end of the jungle to put some distance between you and Jane, distance will undoubtedly become a tyranny.

"It won't be an argument that gets you access to your kids."

It won't be an argument that gets you access to your kids. Rather, it will be learning and applying these three simple rules to your new life. They are a lot easier to understand than your counsel will be at times, or what's going on in court for that matter. Importantly, if the rule 1 problem remains unresolved, even after giving it a real good go, then make sure that your affidavits to the court will show a judge that your lifestyle, the people in it and where you live it are appropriate for your kids. These statements should also focus on when, where and with whom you think your children should spend their time. Ultimately, if you can't agree with Jane, you need to give the judge the best opportunity to grant you some care of your children and in this jungle, time and place mean everything.

2 Be a boy scout

Golden rule 1: 'You both think you're right.'
Golden rule 2: 'Show me you have the time.'
Golden rule 3: 'Show me you have the place.'

Before taking this journey, you need to prepare for what lies ahead. As Aldous Huxley once wrote, 'There are things that are known and there are things that are unknown, and in between are the doors of perception'. Well, given that most fathers who undertake this journey are not solicitors, the 'things that are unknown' will well and truly outweigh the 'things that are known'. If you ignore the three golden rules, most of what you may end up knowing will probably be learned in hindsight. However, what you should already know is what any boy scout can tell you: *be prepared.*

Be prepared for anything, whether you think you know what to expect, you've been told about it, you're unsure or you're completely unaware of what lies ahead. After all, it's a jungle out there. Adopt the boy scouts' motto for this journey, and remember not to pack light, as it could take a while, a long while, to reach the end of this tale. There are many things Tarzan can do to improve his situation. These are what you might call the necessary changes or, as more self-centred people say, 'personal sacrifices' you will need to make for the sake of your children. Never lose sight of your goal, whether or not you are able to see your kids at present, and no matter how thick the jungle may become or how dark some days may seem. It's the uncertainty, the not knowing, that can send Tarzan round the bend and cause his hemotions and man-feelings to erupt like a volcano. So be a boy scout and *be prepared.*

Be prepared for what may be said about you. True or false, it's only words and not sticks or stones. You can't control what Jane will write about you, but if you have prepared properly, hopefully your affidavits will stand up well against hers in court. Don't be reactive, be prepared and plan your way out of the jungle. This means more often than not you'll have to engage your brain and always think before you speak.

Be prepared to be patient. At first Jane may not be agreeable to losing sight of the children, so let patience be your virtue. Worry only about what you need to do. Be dedicated, focused and strategic. Always be polite and courteous, no matter how much it pains you. Be persistent in your efforts, but most of all be prepared to be patient. Good things come to those who wait, and your kids are worth waiting for.

Be prepared for a fight, but don't! It's not constructive or likely to make you any friends, so save your energy for your kids. A spiritual warrior wins without fighting, without getting fired up and hemotional. He doesn't become depressed and disenchanted when the going gets tough, and there's a good chance it will. Always remember, there are not just two but three ways to respond to a challenge. You can choose to answer yes, which is constructive, or no, which is confrontational. Or you can choose the third option and say nothing. That's right, say nothing. Sometimes the best course is not to respond or retaliate. Be prepared to live to fight — or rather not to fight — another day and you'll reach the end of your journey much sooner, which will also be much cheaper than later.

3 Where are the kids?

Golden rule 1: 'You both think you're right.'

Imagine the fear that runs through your body as you search a teeming carnival for your missing children. The desperation and panic that course through your veins. No parent ever wants to feel that fear. Losing a child is unnatural. It's more painful than getting kicked in the nuts, and the hurt doesn't subside with time. We blokes learn to live with discomforts like old football injuries; they don't plague our day, though they can flare up every now and again. Losing sight of Jane may be a blessing, but don't think she won't haunt you, especially if she decides to sink the boot in and make your kids vanish from sight.

"Separating from Jane may or may not have been intentional, but being separated from your children is often uncalled for."

Yes, on close inspection, you'll find that separation or divorce isn't a singular; it's a plural when there's a family involved. Separating from Jane may or may not have been intentional, but being separated from your children is often uncalled for. Losing access to your kids isn't quite like losing them at the show. You probably know exactly where they are, but getting to see them can be another story altogether. Yet the irony of this situation is not lost on you. In a lot of cases Tarzan couldn't care less whether he sets eyes on Jane ever again. All he wants is to see his kids. But he will need at least to speak with Jane in order to do so, and he'll need to find a way to communicate with her in a civil manner. What's even more ironic is you'll need to communicate with Jane in the 'afterlife' much better than you often did during your marriage.

Hurling abuse down the phone does not constitute constructive communication. Neither does making empty threats triggered by desperate hemotions. There's not much point in telling Jane the obvious like, 'You've got my kids' or 'They're my kids too, you ——'. People generally don't respond well to threats of violence or abuse. If you're unsure, pop down to your local DV court for the day. It doesn't matter how much logic there is to your argument; playing with her emotions probably won't change her mind either. Levelling threats like refusing to pay maintenance won't help the situation and is a really bad look in court. There's also the possibility that if you do stop she'll let Family Services know. Whatever you do, please never threaten to take the kids and run. If you do, the only person on the run will be you — from the police.

There is a way to pass the kids' gatekeeper. It's not complicated though many a Tarzan can find it hard. It does take some practice, so best test it out before trying it on her.

Ready, here goes: 'Can I see the kids please?' And remember to smile when you say it. Don't go adding anything else. Just swallow your pride and ask. That's all you need to do. If you think it makes you subordinate to her, just do it for your kids. Surprisingly it often works, because it's simple. More than likely, Jane's answer will be either 'No' or 'When?' That's your cue to name a time and place.

If you get a no, write it down and date it, but don't ask again that day; save it for tomorrow. Know that what you did, regardless of how basic or simple it seems, is the best thing you could have done for two reasons: (1) you showed you care about and want to see your kids, and (2) you didn't fight. Either way there's no harm done, and if Jane refuses to open the gate, your solicitor will most likely present that information to the court.

Being patient and keeping your approach simple and direct offer the fastest route back into your kids' lives. Keeping it civil will overcome any barrier Jane may have erected. Just be prepared and patient, because sooner or later the answer, whether from Jane, her solicitor, a mediator or a judge, will be yes. There's no reason why your most powerful tool in unhitching Jane's wagon can't be persistent politeness.

> "All blokes get knockbacks in the course of their life."

All blokes get knockbacks in the course of their life. Getting one from Jane honestly won't be an overwhelming shock to your system, unlike losing your children at the carnival. They're not really lost, after all; they're simply with their mother. But softly, softly is the way to treat any child and anything related to them. Aussie blokes are hardened by the sun — most of us have been cooked as well — but being a little rounded rather than coarse in your dialogue with Jane will be far better for you and everyone else involved. It doesn't matter what you might think of Jane or her actions. It does matter how you act towards her, though. Being confrontational will ultimately only damage your chances of securing the right to see and care for your children. Keeping it simple and civil will do you, your prospects of seeing your children and your case, whatever it comes to, no harm at all.

4 BRS (Broken Record Syndrome)

Golden rule 1: 'You both think you're right.'

We live in a world of acronyms, where the long-winded is often simplified by a couple of letters. Here's one you may not have come across. BRS relates to one of the most common ailments of any Tarzan who's out on a limb — it's called Broken Record Syndrome. Initially you may think it sounds more like Jane than you, but Broken Record Syndrome is not so much a symptom of behaviour as it is an illness. BRS can strike at the heart of a man, crippling him and destroying his stamina. Going the distance is one thing. Arriving with all your paperwork in order is another.

Really, the only cure for BRS can be found in the diligence with which you maintain your records of contact and conversation with Jane in the afterlife. Perhaps the only positive you can take from another knockback to your efforts to see your kids is the solace that you have recorded and documented Jane's resistance. Without a very good reason or at least a plausible excuse for her behaviour, these records of disappointment may prove to be real positives for your case.

There are, of course, some ifs and buts that go along with this. If you can maintain a civil disposition and not go off at Jane's refusals, then this record of missed parental opportunities will serve your cause. By keeping a log or record of every time this happens, you are building a stronger case for shared care. Often, though, the buts can outweigh the ifs. Consistently reiterating your requests to Jane requires vigilance, but if you press her too often through texting, calling, emailing or tweeting, your persistence may end up looking like a form of harassment. Letting Jane know how much the kids mean to you is one thing, but going over the top may end up doing your case more harm than good.

Copping a 'no' may not be easy, but firing back with your own dose of hurt is only going to destroy any line of communication. Worse still, you may need to explain your actions in a DV (domestic/family violence) court that could result in a civil behaviour order being put in place, which could involve your kids. You may need to repeat yourself more than once to Jane, but do so without sounding like a broken record, whether or not she is hard of hearing.

But really this is not what BRS is about. Maintaining records, no matter what the outcome, is so important in your efforts to win the right to be with your kids. Keeping your cool and maintaining a civil tongue when speaking with Jane is a big, big plus for you. If you are able to show the court a complete, unbroken log of just how many times you have asked Jane to share, it will make it easier for your solicitor when pleading your case. Gaps in your records will only raise questions, but a complete set of statistics will answer more questions than you might realise. If you document all your communications with Jane, make sure you do so consistently, because you don't want anyone asking why you suddenly went missing for a month or two. It might not seem like it at the time, but you are far better off being able to demonstrate that you were knocked back 365 times over 12 months than you are with no records to show for your efforts.

5 Work it, work it

Golden rule 1: 'You both think you're right.'

Old-school thinking about work is that we learn from experience. Hopefully the penny has dropped by now that arguing with Jane will achieve little in return. Starting at the bottom and working your way up the ladder requires a belief in the master–apprentice relationship, where wisdom and experience are the chief informants of an acquired knowledge. Old-school thinking rewards good performance by measuring results over a period of time. Finishing a job by seeing it through to the end, having regard for the detail and taking pride in your work all belong to yesterday. But what is often dismissed as outdated may serve well any Tarzan experiencing less than ideal conditions in the jungle. The more you see securing the care of your children as a job, the better. But those who confuse the idea of parenting itself with a job, stop it. The task at hand is to create the *opportunity* to parent, so it's best to leave the cart behind the horse. By doing this you can also leave the hemotions at home and set about getting this job done.

The more you know what needs to be done, and the less you simply react to situations as they occur, the better off you'll be. Deriving a sense of satisfaction from your day's efforts is rewarding. It can also serve as fuel for the man-engine to motor on when there's still much work to be done. There will be plenty of time to be hemotional after the job is completed, but while there's work to do it's better to apply yourself to the task at hand and save the man-feelings for your kids. Changing the way you view Jane is just as important. It may seem impossible to distance yourself from how she now makes you feel, but if you don't you'll find yourself constantly reacting to her. You have to work with Jane, not against her, if this job is ever going to be manageable. Seeing the new relationship with Jane simply as something you need to manage will certainly reduce the grief in your life.

> "You wouldn't ask an apprentice to do a job they had yet to learn, and the same applies with Jane."

If a parenting agreement is to work on any level, you may as well make it as simple as possible. You wouldn't ask an apprentice to do a job they had yet to learn, and the same applies with Jane. Don't assume she has the skills to manage or perhaps even cope with what's being asked of her. Building a stepped approach to reaching your parenting goals will help you get the job done. Like any situation that looks complicated, planning your approach by breaking the job down into smaller tasks will reduce the risk of failure.

Step 1: *Start agreeing.* By keeping it civil you will be marking out the foundations for agreement.

Step 2: *Start asking.* Request a time and place to see your kids that is manageable for all.

Step 3: *Start making it regular.* Make sure you turn up on time, every time.

Step 4: *Start increasing the time.* Gradually extend the time you spend with your kids.

Step 5: *Start introducing ideas.* Discuss activities you'd like to do with your kids.

Step 6: *Start increasing the frequency.* Inquire about other days of the week you might spend time with them.

Step 7: *Start suggesting overnighters.* Talk about the benefits of having the kids stay over.

"Old-school thinking would suggest you ask someone to do something only if you were prepared to do it yourself."

You may not achieve all seven steps in a week, and some will take longer than others to cement down, but by building in a stepped fashion you are developing a gradual and hopefully reasonable approach to sharing the parenting workload. Old-school thinking would suggest you ask someone to do something only if you were prepared to do it yourself. So the more wisdom you can draw from the good old days of back-breaking labour, the better. Getting to the top requires a fair bit of manoeuvring. Sometimes you need to go back to move forward, or to move at a snail's pace to continue to make progress. But at no time should you drop your bundle or blame your tools. Because the moment you throw in the towel of civilised behaviour you lose sight of the job at hand, the opportunity to parent your kids, and maybe the plot as well.

6 Believe it or not

Golden rule 1: 'You both think you're right.'

Many blokes think mediation is like a CD in a discount bin. It's existence is not necessary and they aren't buying it. But for those who are tighter than a duck's arse, this information will have particular appeal. Believe it or not, the more you can agree the cheaper the costs will be.

Mediation may sound like some form of day surgery or quest for an elusive religious relic, but it's really not uncomfortable or epic. It's actually about helping you reach an agreement so you can get on with the rest of your life. Believe it or not, the job at hand is not to keep on fighting or to 'win' but to find common ground as parents so you can work out an arrangement for the ongoing care of your kids.

> "Where blokes often go wrong is in thinking that mediation is a lightweight or watered down substitute for court."

Where blokes often go wrong is in thinking that mediation is a lightweight or watered down substitute for court. It's not. It's even a requirement of the court. See it for what it really is: the easiest route to working out a solution. Mediation offers you, as a father, a say in shaping the parenting agreement. It's an opportunity for you to make a direct contribution, to influence the outcome. The more positive, organised and observant you are during the mediation process, the better that outcome will be. Personally, the most costly factor in this entire equation is the uncertainty. Uncertainly breeds hemotions that can instigate bad behaviour faster than bacteria grow in your footy socks. Uncertainty stems from fear, and no one likes feeling afraid. So relearning how to reach agreement with Jane will help you in mediation, believe it or not.

Most of us would agree that gaining something, be it tickets in the back row or the chance to spend some time with our children, is better than coming away empty. As a parent, we also want a say in their futures. But in mediation, it's walking; there's definitely no running. To gain an interim parenting agreement — it's probably temporary and may be not exactly what you had hoped for — is still some reward for your efforts to gain parenting equity. It's not the be-all and end-all, but it's a start. Here are 10 simple reasons why it's worth gaining even the most basic mediation agreement:

1. Without one you still have nothing.

2. You will have opened the door for your kids.

3. You will be moving forwards rather than backwards.

4. You can build on it.

5. You can demonstrate your commitment to your kids.

6. You have shown a willingness to be cooperative.

7. You have made some progress in establishing an afterlife with Jane.

8. You have created some rules for you both to follow.

9. You have removed some uncertainty from your children's lives and your own.

10. You have saved a fistful of dollars.

"The other great misconception is that a mediator will take one side over another. This is simply not true."

Mediation is usually only the beginning, but it can be the place to resolve everything and avoid the costs of a lengthy war in the courts. It's not about signing a peace treaty on the first day, but it can be the final resting place of your war. It's more of a test match than a one-dayer, and it can take many sessions to build an agreement. Mediators are long-distance runners and don't give up easily, and neither should you. It's far better to agree to start working on a plan in mediation than it is to tear strips off your children's mother. You need not be alone during mediation. If you can afford legal representation, believe it or not it may be money well spent, especially if it saves you years of ongoing legal bills after your case goes to court.

The other great misconception is that a mediator will take one side over another. This is simply not true. It's far better to be a crewman than the captain of this ship, because you will be required to row in the same direction to find some common ground. It's no secret that the mediator will be trying to find areas of agreement, and will be weighing up your temperament and how much ground you may be willing to give. Ultimately, if the mediator feels unable to reconcile the differences between you, they will issue a certificate advising that your case be resolved in court.

If you can't or won't reach an agreement through mediation, you run the risk of being written up in the mediator's report as disagreeable, unreasonable, argumentative or aggressive, and none of these judgements will benefit you, your case or your kids. Believe it or not, your most cost-effective option is to reach an agreement in mediation before your children's absence begins to bite and the real costs kick in.

7 The waiting game

Golden rule 1: 'You both think you're right.'

Sitting on the sideline can be a lonely place to be. You can feel a little unwanted and left out of the action on field. But you're not alone. If you look around, you should spot a team-mate named Patience who is also waiting for that moment when Jane agrees to share. Playing the waiting game is no fun, but it's something you'll need to learn to do if you're going to make it through the season. There will be times when the wait will seem beyond you and the temptation to pick up the phone and give Jane a spray grows stronger by the day. Unlike a popular sports shoe brand, what's recommended is you just *don't* do it. Be patient. After all, what else can you be?

The waiting may seem like an eternity, but in reality it's not. Patience is more than a card game; it's a matter of will. Live to play another day, or you may find the sideline becomes your permanent position. Worse still, you could end up a spectator in the grandstand and be lost in the crowd.

> "Patience, they say, is a virtue."

Patience, they say, is a virtue, so if it's not something you're recognised for, now may be a good time to work on this aspect of your game. You can't develop patience overnight; that would be a contradiction in terms. It's something you acquire over time, often through testing experiences or situations like this one. You need to be made of the right stuff to exercise restraint and keep your temper and hemotions under control. The better you manage this, the better you will be able to cope with any on-field situations with Jane and as a parent.

Patience will play a role many times in this game, especially when you're waiting for her to recognise your place in the team. The more effort you put in on the training track, the better the result will be come match day, whether you're a starter or not. It's definitely worth revealing this skill to your solicitor, the mediator or the judge. You can't see or smell it, but that doesn't mean you can't show that it's an attribute of your game. After developing it while waiting on the sideline, you need to practise it consistently with Jane. Remember, every knockback you suffer, every insult or slur you choose to ignore, is another run on the scoreboard of tolerance in this game called patience. Record these points on the board, because it's something your solicitor, the mediator or the judge is going to want to see.

But practising patience is not simply about creating scoreboard pressure or racking up points every time Jane says no to your requests to see your kids. It's the way you play the game that's important, because if patience is not on your side you will lose a lot more than you gain. Over the course of the season, if you have consistently practised the patience game, whether or not you're doing much parenting, you will have shown that you have the skills that qualify you to be an important player in your children's lives, and possibly even best on ground.

8 Delaying the inevitable

Golden rule 2: 'Show me you have the time.'
Golden rule 3: 'Show me you have the place.'

Some say there are only two emotions that have the power to make a person act. One is hope, the other fear. They play at either end on the field of human emotions, and each can exert a positive and negative influence over your efforts to secure care of your kids. Which one you decide to use to fuel your tank is your choice, but be warned: when mixed, these two emotions can cause havoc both for you and for your case.

Hope has always been the people's champion. It motivates us and persuades us that the impossible is possible. Fear, on the other hand, has the power to stop us in our tracks, driving us to withdraw and hide in the dressing sheds. Taking this on with fear on your side is like playing from the back foot. Seeing what happens next is not going to score you many runs. Putting your best foot forward and meeting the ball will reduce your chances of being dismissed without playing a stroke.

> "Hope has always been the people's champion. It motivates us and persuades us that the impossible is possible."

If you're looking for an armchair ride on this journey, forget it. It pays not to get too comfortable and anyway chairs have legs, not wheels, so taking a laid-back approach in this situation won't get you far. We all hope something like this will never happen to us, but sitting back and expecting someone else to do all the leg work for you, apart from being lazy, is the act of a man consumed by fear. As paralysing as such fear may feel, it's only an emotion, not a physical disability, so it's not something that should stop you in your tracks. Fear is reactive, but being scared isn't something that should halt your progress. Rather, use it as a warning that you need to bolster your hope by actively seeking support and advice, or by simply summoning up a bit more strength to deal with the situation.

Hope may not always be the friend it claims to be. In any situation it is far better to be driven by hope than by fear, but when hope becomes a single-minded ideal, you'll discover it can lead you astray, because you'll become lost in what you believe rather than what you know. You may be someone who likes to march to the sound of his own drum, but taking the well-travelled road of good advice is far better than being led astray by your own sense of justice.

Used well, hope is inspiring. It can drive you forward in a positive direction and sustain you when you find the going a bit tough. Nourish hope but be a realist, and always listen to your solicitor — that's what you're paying them for. Hope will help you get through this, but don't let it become a back-seat driver, barking out directions. Hope is a great source of energy and personal power, but it is not something you should cling to.

"Believe in yourself, be hopeful and don't let fear paralyse you. Hope will fuel your progress, fear will halt it."

Believe in yourself, be hopeful and don't let fear paralyse you. Hope will fuel your progress, fear will halt it. Be aware of the power of these two emotions, and don't let one lead you astray or the other stop you in your tracks. Be the father who is determined to get the best result for his children, not the one with his head in the sand or, worse, the guy found hiding under a rock somewhere. Leave it too long and your situation will be harder to resolve. But just hoping the problem will fix itself and simply go away is a delusion that you and your children can ill afford.

9 More is more

Golden rule 2: 'Show me you have the time.'
Golden rule 3: 'Show me you have the place.'

It might be cool to say 'less is more' but it's often lazy thinking, and being slack is not going to achieve much that's useful in your situation. Yes, sometimes the more you do the more you muddy the waters, but nothing is simple for a parent, no matter how experienced, competent or caring a Tarzan or Jane may claim to be. When it comes to disputes over the care of children, the only thing you can be sure of is more will be more and less will be less.

The more care of your children you take on, the more you need to do for them. Cases involving more than one child are more often heard in the Family Court than the Federal Magistrates (Circuit) Court, which is a far more expedient place to resolve matters. Some say the Family Court deals with more complicated cases involving children and family assets. These two issues are seen as co-dependent, which is a bit sad rather than shocking or surprising. In divorce or separation proceedings the wealth of the family will generally be allocated so as to provide your kids with security, shelter, care and future life opportunities. Any Tarzan who sees the family wealth as his own because he worked for it can make this known to the court, but it's unlikely to influence the allocation and distribution of family assets. The more care you are awarded, the more assets you are likely to be allocated. The more you earn, however, the less care you may be able to secure and therefore the more you will pay in maintenance. This also means you will receive the lesser amount of the family assets but will probably end up with more time on your hands. What was that about muddied waters?

"Any Tarzan who sees the family wealth as his own because he worked for it can make this known to the court, but it's unlikely to influence the allocation and distribution of family assets."

The more kids involved in the case, the more all this is going to cost. Simply, there will be more to weigh up and write about — perhaps two, three or even four times as many people to consider, each with a developing sense of individuality. Where possible, the courts prefer that children are not separated. If you have older kids, their opinions will also be considered and may in fact determine or at least influence care arrangements.

Older brothers and sisters provide younger siblings with security, especially in times of uncertainty and change. This is just one reason why it's not good to split them up, but often this concession is made through consent, which highlights the key role of compromise in any solution. Concerns regarding care vary with the age and number of children, along with the value, influence and role of each parent. Maintaining established relationships and establishing or, in many cases, re-establishing relationships between a parent and children may be dealt with differently. But rest assured, the court is looking for an uncomplicated solution, one that is least likely to be contravened by either party.

More will be more when, as a single parent, you look at the costs of providing a suitable environment for your children. As a parent and provider you should be familiar with this, as you have had to dig deeper into your hip pocket for each successive child. Trying to provide for all on a single wage becomes mathematically increasingly difficult. Arriving at an agreed arrangement is far more beneficial both for the kids and for your finances.

The more children you have the more agreeable you need to be, as there are simply more issues to address and therefore more that can go wrong. It's possible too that the more children you have the more it's going to hurt. So again, the more you can resolve amicably without the assistance of the courts, the less painful it's going to be for everyone. In a sense, then, there is some truth to the idea of less being more. You can either 'pay less and agree more' or 'agree less and pay more'. For those who remain defiant and uncooperative, the risk of paying more and having less time with their kids will become much greater.

"The more children you have the more agreeable you need to be, as there are simply more issues to address and therefore more that can go wrong."

10 What's mine is now yours

Golden rule 2: 'Show me you have the time.'
Golden rule 3: 'Show me you have the place.'

You may have broken your back for years to make a dollar to support your family, and the family may have provided significant support to enable you to bring home the bacon. But when it comes to the dollars and cents of separation, the main provider cannot expect a refund or count on being awarded the majority of the family assets. Even if you weren't married, or you had lived together little more than six months, the Family or Federal Magistrates (Circuit) Court will want the assets of the relationship valued before deciding how they will be disbursed. As much as we are told relationships are 50/50, when it comes to dividing up the pot you will need to swallow a bitter pill: 'equity' is not based on percentages. Losing your kids is hard enough, but losing what you have worked for is enough to push a man over the edge. Understanding how it works won't necessarily bring you any comfort, but at least it will give you some idea of what may be in store and how you can best prepare.

The Family Law Act values the contributions of the supporter as much as it does the breadwinner in a relationship. These days dual incomes are the norm, or rather a necessity. But even if Jane sat at home watching the soaps while the kids were at school and you were at work, the rule of thumb on the distribution of assets of the relationship may not account for the blood, sweat and tears that either party contributed to the partnership. Even your super, though not accessible for many years, could be calculated in the mix.

This process of consideration and allocation of assets, cash and investments is not something that popped up overnight. It has evolved since the mid-1970s and the introduction of the *Family Law Act,* and it takes into account the reality that often the concerned parties find it difficult to agree. What you may consider to be 'just' is probably not what the court will consider 'fair'. And yes, it is unreasonable to think that a judge will favour one party over the other. There are many factors the court will need to consider; rest assured, though, its decisions will take into account the past but will be made for the future, whether you like it or not. How the court does this is no great secret.

There's no simple formula or rule of thumb that can be applied to such complex matters. However, there are four major steps the court will take before ruling on the distribution of the material wealth of your relationship. These are: (1) totalling the assets of the relationship, (2) assessing the contributions of each party, (3) understanding the future needs of each party, and (4) making a decision that is fair and equitable for both Tarzan and Jane.

1. In calculating the sum of the assets of the relationship, the court will consider all assets as belonging to the relationship, even if they were purchased or the investments made prior to the relationship. Arguing that your boat is yours alone is a complete waste of energy and the court's time. It may not seem just or fair, but that's how it is, so be prepared.

2. In assessing the contributions of each party, the court will consider who owned what in the beginning and what each party contributed during the term of the relationship. Although at the beginning of the relationship contributions may have been one-sided (you or Jane may have owned a car or a house, for instance), this is considered to be only the starting point from which the court will work. The longer the relationship lasted, the more likely it is that non-cash contributions to the relationship will balance things out. The court doesn't put a price on the financial support or the day-to-day care of the kids; rather, it values the contributions and recognises the nature of co-dependency in the relationship. You may think taking your lunch to work was saving the family money, but when it comes to splitting up the assets, the efforts of the sandwich maker will be considered, regardless of how bland or unimaginative your cheese and Vegemite lunches were in hindsight.

3. In determining future needs, the court will consider the age and the future earning capacity of each party. It may consider the amount of support given to either party in the relationship, for instance to help one or the other to obtain qualifications that increased his or her earning capacity, or who has predominantly cared for the kids. This is where percentages, as opposed to dollar figures, are used to ensure that the respective contributions to the relationship are recognised in the final distribution. The larger the total sum of the family's assets, the lower the percentage that may be applied. The smaller the estate, the greater the percentage may be. For instance, if the assets total a million dollars, then a correction or adjustment of 10% would equal $100,000. But if the total assets were $100,000, then 10% would be only $10,000. Therefore, a larger percentage might need to be applied to achieve a fair outcome, in the court's view. Again, there is no rule for determining the adjustment, but rest assured, it will be made.

4. In determining what is fair, the court may consider the borrowing potential of each party in the future. The court seeks to provide each party with an opportunity to lead a reasonable lifestyle after the distribution of assets. So again it will take account of who has the means to make money and who has the kids. Often the court will give the party with the greatest earning capacity, and therefore the largest borrowing potential, less than the party who may not have the power to obtain significant credit in the future. The court's aim is not to leave one party destitute and the other 'living the life of Riley', but rather to ensure that after the separation each party has a more or less equal opportunity in their new life.

The more you consider the above four steps that guide the Family Court's decision making on distributing family assets, the more you may be able to reduce your perceived losses. That said, if there are items of particular personal value to you, you are better off walking out the door with them under your arm, as it is often the case that things of sentimental value may simply disappear, be broken (preferably not over your head) or not be considered to be of any great value by the court. So if fishing keeps you sane, take your rods and don't forget the boat, because what you might find is, what was yours could be up for sale.

11 Some things change and some stay the same

Golden rule 2: 'Show me you have the time.'
Golden rule 3: 'Show me you have the place.'

If you still don't understand why your popularity plummets every time you try to make your favourite footy socks see out the working week, you're going to struggle with this idea. Change is something that happens all around us every second of the day. Yes, trees do fall in the jungle, whether you see them or not. If you're still unsure about that, take a walk in the bush and see how many trees grow horizontally. Change is like medicine. Even when it leaves a bad taste in your mouth, it's still good for you. If you avoid taking your medicine like a man, you may also be avoiding what could be the biggest change of your adult life.

"When everything appears to be spinning out of control, try to stand still like a rock and see where things fall."

A very wise man once said, 'When everything appears to be spinning out of control, try to stand still like a rock and see where things fall'. In your current situation this advice, like the judge's, is pure gold. To 'stand still' means to observe rather than react to what is going on around you. The fewer ripples you make on the water, the fewer waves you'll create. Don't allow the hemotions to run wild or begin throwing the bat at every delivery. You're better off keeping your thoughts about Jane and her behaviour to yourself when occupying the crease, keeping a straight bat and playing each ball on its merits. Watching carefully what's going on will make change easier to spot and help you deal with it more effectively. There's no rule or law that says change can't be of some benefit to you.

Remember, patience is a virtue in this process. Change happens in its own time and place, so the longer you maintain your patience and follow due process, the greater the chances that the change you are seeking will occur. Don't rush the process or force the issue, because you may not be able to afford a second innings. Observing Jane's answers will be far better for you and your kids than simply reacting to them. Listening to good advice and taking it on board is a far better approach than just demanding your own way. The change you are seeking lies in your willingness to contribute to an agreement, which may take time, especially if Jane needs to change her behaviour too.

Change is difficult to accept and even harder to enforce, and it becomes near impossible to establish if you resort to fighting. You won't be the only one whose world is changing. Your children's world will also look very different, but no matter where things fall, and despite what anyone says, writes or reads about you, they will remain your children, you will remain their father and Jane is always going to be their mother. Regardless of how divided their family has become, your children will always remain your family.

> "Change is difficult to accept and even harder to enforce, and it becomes near impossible to establish if you resort to fighting."

If you can't build some sort of agreement from the pieces of your relationship once the dust has settled, then the court will do its best to do so for you. Just be aware, a court order will have a degree of permanency to it. So much can change in your life. And you can bet that unless the storm has subsided and the wind has stopped blowing, more change is on its way. Hopefully at least some of this change will be for the better, and one way to ensure this is to remain still so you can see where things fall. Be the rock and let your actions be an example to all. The more you observe, the more you'll see what's really going on. Listening to advice may be a change from your usual modus operandi but it may help you create order out of the chaos. Once you've done so you'll be good to go, and the real change in your life will be knowing what the future looks like for you and your children.

12 The best-laid parenting plans of mice and men

Golden rule 2: 'Show me you have the time.'
Golden rule 3: 'Show me you have the place.'

A parenting plan is written on paper, not rubber, so don't bend the rules. It may weigh next to nothing, but its contents are likely to be set in stone. Looking at it for the first time, it's hard to see where the money's gone, yet what you're looking at is a game plan that defines how things are going to be now and into the future. It may be written in plain English, but it often doesn't read that way. The legal meanings of key words in these kinds of documents are of consequence.

There's no simple formula or template to explain how these documents are built, and those who will be governed by them may end up not making a single contribution to their construction. *The Family Law Act 1975* makes *War and Peace* seem like a Sunday afternoon read. What may be easier to get your head around are the amendments that were introduced in 2006. It is known that as prime minister, John Howard felt that fundamental changes to the Family Law Act were needed if single fathers were to be more than just people their children visited on a weekend.

"Yes, paper can be folded, but these rules are not to be bent."

Be assured, if separation does occur a parenting order is almost unavoidable. So again, the more you act to create an agreement the less costly it will be for all. Yes, paper can be folded, but these rules are not to be bent, so it's best to put it all out on the negotiating table, rather than trying to have it amended a couple of weeks, months or years later. Dates and times in a document like this are concrete and should be rigorously adhered to. The order may also define how, when and where you are obliged to communicate with Jane about the care and maintenance of the children. If arguing is in your genes, it will also spell out how you are to behave towards each other. Don't worry about how shallow the gene pools are that you or Jane may have come from. The amendments to the Family Law Act have considered the lowest possible common dominators in reshaping this law to create a more equitable parenting outcome for children.

Two expressions that carry significant weight in parenting orders are 'lives with' and 'spends time with'. These words will identify the primary carer, so don't make the assumption that 'shared' means equal. A shared care arrangement may initially be proposed to you and Jane, but if for one or a multitude of reasons you can't find common ground, the sharing suggestion may quickly evaporate from the conversation. The court now considers shared care arrangements to be best, but ultimately, if relations remain hostile, what is best for the kids is that you or Jane may end up with what's called vaguely 'significant time'. No one is really sure how long 'significant time' is meant to be. So your availability to your children may determine how much 'significant time' you could be afforded. Hopefully it will include consecutive days during the week and over the weekend.

The biggest no-no is to waste your time and that of others trying to help you by breaking these orders at any stage. Before you decide that ditching the rules is okay, think about these two factors:

1. Contravening your order can be seen as criminal and attract fines and charges.

2. The court may revisit and tighten those orders faster than you can get down on your knees and plead for leniency.

> "After all, the order is made to help Tarzan and Jane to create continuity and equity for their children."

That said, the court is not unreasonable, but your excuse for deviating from any orders better be extremely good. After all, the order is made to help Tarzan and Jane to create continuity and equity for their children. In the end it may appear to be pretty simple, as it probably could have been all along, but most of the time simplicity is what's needed to ensure a parenting order is workable. Orders aren't made to accommodate hemotions, or shemotions for that matter. They are there to help Tarzan or Jane maintain a civil and equitable parenting relationship. If Jane has the kids and tries to resist a mutual resolution, don't fret, because if she is reluctant to share there's a good chance the parenting order will insist that she does.

13 Hand over the children

Golden rule 2: 'Show me you have the time.'
Golden rule 3: 'Show me you have the place.'

Handing over your children, even to Jane, can be difficult for any Tarzan. It may be something you dread or feel is just plain wrong, and you may be right; it is unnatural, but according to Australia's family lore of the jungle it happens every day. As an emotional experience it leaves you cold and with a lonely ride home, but it's often mandatory and just one of the unpleasant experiences you go through as a single parent. It often takes place in a public space in front of many witnesses. A rule of thumb is to always tread lightly and leave quietly. It may be uncomfortable saying goodbye to your children in front of Jane, so often it's best to have that conversation before the handover. It's also a time when your kids are exposed to the nature of your afterlife with their mother. Never have a go at Jane, insulting or belittling her, especially in the presence of your kids. After all, why should they endure such childish games, when their parents are supposed to be the adults?

Never, ever, ever be late to drop them off or pick them up. The first thing Jane will think is you've done a runner or she'll start practising her 'You don't care enough about your kids' rant. Traffic isn't an excuse, so where you live can be either helpful or a handicap and a sign that you're not as organised as you need to be. If you are stuck in gridlock on the highway, then a phone call or text is far better than an excuse once you arrive. Equally, it's not really a great idea to rub it in when she's late — just note it down in the log. Five minutes is nothing, and even an hour can be forgiven. Cutting Jane some slack may also pay a dividend in the future. It's always going to be better to greet her with a 'Good to see you' than with 'I've been waiting for . . .' How you manage the atmosphere at handover is critical to making your parenting order work, and the more you keep it civil and agreeable, the easier the arrangement will be to maintain.

To put it simply, keep it about the kids in these situations. The less you dwell on what went wrong in your relationship, the less likely you are to start an argument. Spend this time discussing your children's needs or how they are doing at school, rather than letting them hear how big you think their mother's mouth is. Asking to move the goalposts, repeatedly, is not a good look to the court and is a sign that what suits you, comes first. You may feel you had to compromise unreasonably to meet the terms of the parenting order, but it's always in the best interests of your children to maintain them to the letter.

It's never going to be a picnic or even a fun experience. The order won't last forever, but Jane is going to be your kids' mother for some time to come. It's best to etch your parenting order into the non-negotiables of your week, because you may have had to work pretty hard to get it set up in the first place. It's discipline, not man-feelings, that will serve you best as you hop to this not so merry dance in the years to come. You'll always be far better off not stepping on anyone's toes, no matter how many times you're to do this jig.

14 The lore of the jungle

Golden rule 2: 'Show me you have the time.'
Golden rule 3: 'Show me you have the place.'

'Hey Tarzan, how's it hanging?' asks his primate friend.

'You can see, it's touching the ground,' replies Tarzan.

'Where's Jane and the kids?' asks his friend.

Tarzan winks and says, 'Jane's at home, looking after the little monkeys.'

Unfortunately, guys, the joke, which is not at all funny, is on us. Fast forward to the middle of the 20th century, and you won't find Tarzan and his primates hanging out in a tree. That's because pubs have been invented. But Jane's still at home when Tarzan comes swinging through the front door, hoping she has the dinner on. Even if we get all medieval about it, with Tarzan wearing shining armour and galloping around slaying dragons while Jane is locked up in the castle at home with the kids. Since time began, it doesn't matter what era in history you choose, the ending has always been the same. Tarzan provides and Jane cares.

This is not to say that men can't, won't or don't care for their kids. The lore that was written way back in the jungle and has pretty much been the norm for humans for tens of thousands of years reads: women care and men provide for the family. Every bloke who has ever gone out into the world to make his mark, or prove something to his father, has upheld this lore without the slightest premonition of how it might come to affect fathers in the early 21st century.

> "Although it is not set in stone, written in the law books or scrawled in the court toilets, the unspoken lore of nature is very much part of the concrete jungle."

This lore of the jungle is easily observed in nature, so it's not really something our forefathers had much control over. As they say these days, it's in our genes. Whether or not we choose to blame Tarzan for it, the issues of today simply won't go away. Divorce and separation are on the rise and although we have known how to earn a shekel since Tarzan played halfback for the Cheetahs, displaying our abilities in the arena of caring for children has not been a historically natural thing for blokes to do. But we can and, in times like these, more often than not we need to.

Although it is not set in stone, written in the law books or scrawled in the court toilets, the unspoken lore of nature is very much part of the concrete jungle. It is admirable for any man to want to take out the hammer and chisel in order to become a carer, but we don't write down this type of natural lore. They're already inscribed in our DNA.

When you realise that this lore is known to the courts, the idea that shared care is a 50/50 deal and that 'everything is equal' doesn't seem so real. But how could it, when everyone who's come before, up to and including those who are there on your day in court, has instinctively lived by this lore? And there is no scientific theory or expert opinion that is going to convince anyone of anything different. Asking Google for help reveals it to be as artificially knowledgeable as it is useless. This is a mother of a problem, but us blokes also come from mother nature, and she did not forget to equip men with the tools for caring, even if many of us don't know where they are, what they are for or how to use them.

"This is a mother of a problem, but us blokes also come from mother nature, and she did not forget to equip men with the tools for caring."

Being a provider is a bit easier than being green, but not much. Knowing how, and doing it week in week out, is a real skill, especially when it comes to creating a suitable environment and opportunities for your kids. We also should instinctively know how to give good advice, be a guiding light or provide a helping hand. You don't have to tell a man it's a good thing we aren't women, but no matter how skilled we are in the art of providing, we often forget how this skill can also be applied in different forms of caring. Though we may be accused of being heavy-handed at times, and may look awkward holding newborn babies, men do care for children and have done so for thousands of years. If Tarzan doesn't remember the milk, it doesn't mean he's an irresponsible parent. You know he'll go back and get it, even if he has to fight off a couple of lions and the odd cougar along the way.

THE ANIMAL KINGDOM

15 Personal enemy number one

Golden rule 1: 'You both think you're right.'

The biggest war you'll wage in all this madness won't be with Jane, the Dragon, the army of the dead or the system; it will be the war with yourself. The greatest damage you do to yourself, your case, your relationships and, most of all, your kids will not be inflicted by the wrath of Jane or an expensive barrister who is trying to hang you out to dry by airing your dirty laundry in court. It will come from you, and from no one else. All your actions and behaviour, throughout what is arguably one of the most difficult challenges of your life, are actually within your control, if you remain disciplined and keep your hemotions in check.

How you conduct yourself during this frustrating and emotionally painful period is ultimately what you will be judged on. If your case does go to court for consideration, you can be sure that your conduct during these trying times will inform the judge's decision. You can also be sure that the judge will bring to your case a far broader and more experienced perspective than yours. This may or may not be your first time down this road — it can happen more than once in a lifetime — but judges deal with these kinds of issues for a living.

The court assesses your situation not simply based on your version, perspective or understanding of events and behaviour; it will also consider Jane's viewpoint and possibly the views of friends and family from both sides of the fence, the police, psychologists, psychiatrists and mediators. So how you appear and conduct yourself to the many, not just your kids, will ultimately inform the decision that is made. It's not a talent show. Juggling fire doesn't really impress anyone these days. Your behaviour and actions during these testing times will be evaluated, though. Patience will score well, as will a father who demonstrates a dedication and commitment to being a responsible and active parent.

It's not a popularity contest, but it is advisable to enlist allies, rather than allowing your opponent to dominate the field. You don't have to impress so much as to press upon people your commitment to parenting your children. Remember, you're not the only one carrying an emotional burden. The various professionals you encounter along the way will be detached from your situation and will favour your sober observations and comparisons over hemotions any day of the week. Maintain your dignity and convey your respect for the responsibilities of fatherhood. Because the resolution of your case may well influence the cases of many fathers to come.

Maintain your focus and keep it about the kids. You don't need to sell yourself so much as to demonstrate your parental commitment and responsibility towards your kids. Above all, don't fight with anyone, especially yourself. Rather, be the cooperative one, the one who is willing to share, to act impartially and responsibly. So don't go beating yourself up, or anyone else for that matter, because you don't need to fight to win this war.

16 The Spiritual Warrior vs the Ultimate Fighter

Golden rule 1: 'You both think you're right.'

In the red corner, weighing in at (insert Jane's weight) and fighting out of the former family home is the unreasonable one. Weighing in and trying to negotiate their way out of the blue corner is the one who wants a fight. If this is how you see things, even if you have a dozen Golden Gloves and a couple of world titles under your belt, going toe to toe won't help your cause. It doesn't matter how much Jane sledged you in the pre-match press conference, the reality is it takes two to fight. If you're able to resist being goaded into one, you may be surprised by the result. Swinging punches, throwing objects, slandering and bickering may well be traits of Jane, but if you're to have a chance of gaining care of your children, adopting this sort of behaviour will not help your case.

Despite all the pain and hardship Jane may be inflicting on you, taking up your parenting cause as if it was a heavyweight decider is a big no-no. Regardless of all the name calling and threats that 'you'll never see your kids again', do not don the gloves. No matter how much you think you have lost or have been hurt, stop entertaining ideas of staging a rematch, because fighting doesn't solve anything. It simply perpetuates problems. Jane may not be willing to split the family assets down the middle and share the care, but you don't need to fight with her to be a parent. Fighting is likely to a major reason why you are separated, and carrying on like a prize-fighter could further alienate you from your kids, which is not what you want to achieve.

> "The real battle of the Spiritual Warrior is the one waged with the universal enemy of self-ignorance."

Understand this: fighting with Jane will not work; it will only create a bigger, more expensive mess for everyone involved. The truth is, as much as you might like this to be a ding-dong battle, it isn't. As much as you might see Jane as public enemy number one, she isn't. Again, the truth is there is actually no one to contest with and the only fight you're likely to have is with yourself. You'll want to think you're fighting for your kids, but it may be your sanity that's really on the line. Muhammad Ali was full of great one-liners, but none of them will help you in this situation. And Rocky is not the role model you're looking for. Somewhere between lover and fighter is the pragmatic peacemaker, and although this may not sound like a glamorous role, it could produce a far better result for you and your children.

Tibetan Buddhists believe in the power of the Spiritual Warrior, the one, they say, who fights without fighting. The real battle of the Spiritual Warrior is the one waged with the universal enemy of self-ignorance, the ultimate source of personal suffering. The Spiritual Warrior's main weapons are to act with compassion and to help others develop wisdom. This way the Spiritual Warrior really has no enemy other than his own lack of understanding or knowledge, which can be practically addressed. Rather than an external enemy, like Jane, the Spiritual Warrior battles within to rid the self of flaws and failings. In a sense, to be the Spiritual Warrior means taking a good hard look in the mirror to see where the problem lies, rather than looking for a fight.

The one thing that can undo an Aussie guy is uncertainty. Not knowing where your children are can be very unnerving and can easily lead to an outpouring of hemotions. Resolution is what you're looking for, not an eruption, so it's far better to be a warrior than a knockout artist. The monk Chogyam Trungpa put it best when he said, '*Warriorship* does not refer to making war on others. Aggression is the source of our problems, not the solution'. To the Tibetans the strength of warrior is not in his ability to make war. It is more closely related to the word *pawo*, which means 'one who is brave'. Taking a good hard look at oneself is far braver act than simply throwing a punch. If a father needs to be anything, he needs to be brave. Brave enough to ask the hard questions and to resist reacting to Jane's abuse.

It's not an axe that you need to wield, and armour won't protect you. It's your heart that you need to make visible and to wear so all can see. Your children are a matter of the heart, and at the end of the day that's why it hurts. Paying attention to your bruised ego is one thing, but being swayed by its recommendations is not the approach of the Spiritual Warrior. To fight the good fight without fighting, you must remain vigilant and focused on your kids, not on Jane. To be brave is to own the mistakes of your past and to face up to the challenges that may be thrown at you.

But the best piece of advice from your corner comes from a fox in a small book called *The Little Prince* who rightfully says, 'Only with the heart can one see rightly, what is essential is invisible to the eye'. The only fight we need to have is not with Jane, or anyone else, but with our own ignorance. After all, fighting with Jane is about as useful and effective as shadow-boxing in the dark.

"The only fight we need to have is not with Jane, or anyone else, but with our own ignorance."

17 Buck up little camper

Golden rule 2: 'Show me you have the time.'
Golden rule 3: 'Show me you have the place.'

As isolating as this experience feels, know you're not alone. Though it's tempting to see your story as a horror, tragedy, thriller or comedy, don't let it become a drama. Help for a single father is scarce. There are men's groups you can join, websites you can visit and of course help lines you can ring. Unfortunately none of these are going to change your situation. That challenge falls fairly and squarely on your shoulders, whether or not you think they're wide enough to carry the load. Buck up little camper, because you'll need to if you're to make it out of this jungle.

The old 'light at the end of the tunnel' is just that: a brighter place that's some distance away. Your current problems can make you feel like it's groundhog day every day, but realistically, if you're prepared to do the hard yards, you should be looking at 18 to 24 months, tops. This might seem like a long time but that can also be a blessing in disguise. There are likely to be many changes you'll need to make over the stretch. Building your case won't take as long as Rome, but apart from your solicitor it's you who will need to do much of the ground work.

Time gives the space for change to occur, and obviously that's what you're aiming for. Don't be surprised if Jane needs some prodding to come round to a willingness to share parental responsibilities. Often time is what's needed for this to happen. Again, it's time and a fair bit of humility that are needed when a graduated care arrangement is negotiated. Whether or not you agree it's necessary, buck up little camper and do it for your kids.

There may be times when you pine for the good old days and the way things used to be. Children complicate things, especially relationships. They don't mean to, they just do. Unless you have recently purchased a time machine, your memories are probably the only thing you will revisit. But take heart from knowing that every day you are a little bit closer to putting this to bed, hopefully along with your kids. Though it pays to keep your head down, the truth is it won't be like this forever.

> "There may be times when you pine for the good old days and the way things used to be."

The more you do to improve your situation to care for your children, the faster that day will come. Timing is everything and by the time everything is in place (and it needs to be), you'll wonder at how quickly it flew by. If you've got your head in your hands now, then you're not doing much more than worrying. Worse still, you're not doing anything to fix the situation. Buck up little camper because improving your life while Jane remains uncooperative is the best thing you can do for your kids, whether they see this or not.

18 Divided and conquered

Golden rule 1: 'You both think you're right.'

Separation is the root of all parenting problems. Gone are the days when you heard, 'Honey, can you look after the kids while I pop down the road'. There might be a whole lot of other things you don't have to listen to these days as well. But Jane will always be the mother of your children and you still need to manage the afterlife with her, for better or worse. Separation can mean independence and freedom or it can create a sense of isolation and imprisonment. Put simply, it's a very big change on a not so grand scale. Personally it can gut a man, see old habits reintroduced, cause internal conflict and drive a bloke to drink.

Your kids now have a divided family and, potentially, a damaging parental imbalance. Relationships can be tested in times when you are without contact, but there may be little you can achieve before you get to court. In the grander scheme, the situation is only temporary and will not ruin the years to come. Just don't let things sit in the too-hard basket for too long. Access issues are nothing more than a barrier erected by Jane, though it could be electrified or seem 20 foot high. Again this is only temporary, and you can look forward to the times that lie ahead when you and the kids are reunited.

Man-feelings or hemotions are just distractions, but they can lead to outbursts of abuse or violence. Don't let them rule your house, no matter how empty it seems right now, or they will tear you down and your case apart. If the memory is full and you need to download, do it out of reach of your mobile and out of earshot of Jane and your kids. A counsellor may be a cost-effective outlet and a good source of advice if you don't want to burden family members with another crisis update. Men's sheds and groups can also be places of solace and personal advice. Just remember, you can't be conquered if you don't engage in battle.

The independence you may have sought, or have been given, should allow you to disengage even though the enemy may still be hostile. Leave the arguments to the 'when we were together' time and allow your afterlife with Jane to proceed without the aggro, at least from your side. Aggression is a waste of your energy, it doesn't look good on any record and ultimately it will hurt your children. Let the judge see the example you set as a father.

As divided as you and Jane have become, it is beneficial to your kids if you tolerate a little or even a lot of irate behaviour in this new era. If the lines are down, it may be time to seek advice, summon up a bit more patience or just wait a week for the full moon to pass. Ultimately you know her best — which buttons work and which buttons not to press. Being divided may turn out to be a blessing in disguise. Remember, the conquered all chose to fight but despite their best efforts came up short of the line. Even if the kitchen sink does get hurled at you, if there's no fight there will be no winner, and that way your children won't end up losers either.

19 Thank you

Golden rule 1: 'You both think you're right.'

Arthur Herbert Fonzarelli, Fonzie to his mates, was cool. He was so cool his only flaw was his inability to admit he was ever wrong. At times he tried to admit his faults but often struggled to pronounce the word, offering little more than a slurring of sounds. For most of a sitcom that ran and re-ran for decades, Fonzie was never wrong, partly because he was a bloke and partly because he was the personification of cool. Like many Australian single fathers you may have a leather jacket in the closet, but a black coat alone won't help you keep your cool during these times.

Conceding that some of your past actions may have been wrong is being honest. It might be an admission on your part that you're fallible, but it may also be something that Jane believes and knows is true. Recognising in your court affidavits that you're not the Fonz but just a man is not going to hurt you or your case. It could simply show that you recognise where things went wrong and point towards the more conciliatory road you are seeking to travel. You can't change the past, but you can change your ways now.

If you are to gain a shared care arrangement you may also need to mend some bridges. Letting Jane know might even soften her stance, though it's unwise to use this time to reunite, because chances are, if separated occurred once, there's a likely chance it will happen again. 'Thank you' is a word — well it's really two — that if pronounced clearly could prove to be very valuable to your cause. It could require some practice and you may experience Fonz-itis, but mastering this tongue twister is a must. What's cool is being a great dad to your kids, and one way to unlock this box is by using the words 'thank you'. The chance to deliver this simple chant may not present itself at once, but when timed well it can soften the most hardened heart. Finding a context may tempt you towards sarcasm to begin with: you could thank her for the debt or the pain and suffering. But the sooner the opportunity arises to thank her for letting you see the kids again, the sooner the next time is likely to be.

> "Be thankful."

While you can't change the past, neither can Jane. Often people continue doing the wrong thing because it's easier than admitting to a mistake. It may be her solicitor or a court order that advises or directs Jane to share the parenting of your kids. Be thankful. Use the opportunity to thank her for any and every concession she makes, whether you think she deserves it or not. You obviously don't appreciate all she's done for you, and it may not have been nearly enough, but every chance you get, no matter how small, give thanks. After all, it could be worse. You could have been married to Fonzie, and then you'd be stuck with someone who might never admit they too could be wrong.

20 On your side

Golden rule 1: 'You both think you're right.'

Believe it or not, there are people on your side. Some of them may have fallen into line voluntarily; others you may have picked to do a job. Some will have gone missing in action; others may be sitting on the fence, and then there are those who have defected to the dark side. Luckily this is not a game of numbers, but as long as you have the right players in key positions, you should be prepared for whatever comes your way. You can be guaranteed it will come, in some cases by the bucket load. Although they say mud doesn't stick, if Jane is going to sling it some probably will; don't sweat it, just find someone who's prepared to hose you down.

> "Even if you're Billy the Kid, taking aim and firing at will is not going to bring this tale to a happy ending anytime soon."

You may have plenty of ammunition of your own, but seriously think twice before entering into a slinging match. Even if you're Billy the Kid, taking aim and firing at will is not going to bring this tale to a happy ending anytime soon. You might win a few points, but here's the news: no one's keeping score. If you come out all guns blazing you may run out of steam before the smoke clears. And here's the biggest twist: even if you can hit a target from a hundred paces, the truth is you can't hit a ghost. And that's what you are really fighting — the ghost of your relationship.

Some of your friends and acquaintances may have switched camp, but hurling abuse at them, even if they are meddling in your affairs, won't gain you anything. They are likely to have skeletons in their own closets and may be no saints, but taking offense will only create the impression that you're the one who's looking for a fight or has something to hide. Neither of these qualities score highly in the game of parenting. Win, lose or draw, they are simply of no benefit to your case. You are better off sticking to the rules, playing your own game, and clearly demonstrating that your behaviour is contrary to the fan mail from Jane or her army of the dead.

The less you fish at balls outside your off stump that won't get you out, the more your form will improve and the better the result will be. It's only when you get drawn into a false shot or start sledging that the mud will stick. But when ignored, such a ball is often seen by the umpire for what it really is, and that's wide of the mark. You're better off watching it go through to the keeper or at least seeing how much heat is really on it before you play a shot. Sure, if it's there for the hitting, dispense it to all corners of the park. But don't make a habit of chasing the loose stuff, because you'll lose sight of your goal and eventually end up being caught out.

There will be those who claim not to be on anyone's side, though eventually everyone ends up barracking for one side over another. Remember, a fair game is a good game in the court and in mediation. The biggest mistake you can make with any official before, during or after the game is to harbour suspicions that they are having a quiet wager on the other side. Quickly retire that thought for the rest of the match, because you don't want to be giving off this perception or making accusations. Apart from raising questions about people's professionalism and bringing the game into disrepute, it will only lead to more arguments. Accusing the umpire of match fixing is ill-advised and will not win you any friends, or fans for that matter.

> "Being drawn into someone else's argument will only make your efforts seem defensive."

There's always a bit of showmanship that goes on during court proceedings, but injecting yourself into the game and coming to the attention of the referee is not a great idea. Rest assured, they will not hesitate to blow the whistle and award a penalty that will cost you more than a week's suspension on the sidelines. Even to be seen arguing the point with officials is not a good look and could give an unnecessary advantage to the opposition. Sticking to you structured game plan and remaining positive are keys if you want to make it to the end of the season. Being drawn into someone else's argument will only make your efforts seem defensive. You won't achieve a personal best by running someone else's race. You are far better off investing your efforts in marshalling your own troops than entertaining the opposition's sledging. If you're aware of the boundaries, you'll be less likely to cross them. If you know where the vantage line is, you won't concede ground unnecessarily. And if you avoid an all-in, you may escape the sin bin and a penalty that could decide the game.

21 Family tree

Golden rule 2: 'Show me you have the time.'
Golden rule 3: 'Show me you have the place.'

It's a good thing you don't get to pick your family, if your relationship with Jane is anything to go by. Blood is thicker than water and if you ever wanted to put this theory to the test, now is your opportunity. Within your family you may find all the support you need, which will save you burdening your mates and jeopardising other friendships. Family, after all, is what you make of it, and in this situation what yours make of you can be of massive benefit to your case.

If family is ever worth its weight in gold, it's when one of its members comes under fire. When the salt is tested there will be those who stand up or at least stay nearby, and there will be those who flee. Either way, they are your family and hopefully still consider you in the same light. Now is the time to remember every little favour you have done them and redeem as many IOUs as possible. Rest assured, whatever capacity they have, families will always go to bat for one of their own. So even if you're out of favour with some family factions, take heart in knowing they will still be fond of your kids.

Dads are more useful for financial support than wisdom in these matters. Even if they have already walked this path, the jungle is very different these days. The quiet word or gesture of reassurance is what these blokes are specialists in. So take the time to listen to their often rare words, whether or not there's wisdom in them. No one understands you as well as your mother and guardian angel. Not only is she a source of parental knowledge and wisdom, but she is potentially your most powerful asset. She alone may possess the power to ease a judge's doubts or silence Jane's slurs. She is also your children's grandmother, and though she has no legal claim to your kids, she, like your father, will usually have a very significant relationship with them.

Your sister, if you are lucky enough to have one, can be a feminine voice of sanity and reason. If she has kids of her own, both she as aunty and her kids, your children's cousins, could play a vital role in supporting your position as a father. A brother and his family may play a similar role. They too may be willing to provide supervision during visits, or at least offer a good word. Your brothers and sisters will also know what you need to hear to stay emotionally afloat on this treacherous sea, or will throw you a life vest or provide a blanket and a couch for the night.

Families might not always be cool, but fashion and fast cars aren't much use to you when you're faced with a station wagon reality. Families can be pillars of strength offering loyalty, wisdom, home-cooked meals and good advice. Make of them what we will, they don't come from the video store, so returning them is not an option. Find some solace in the familiarity of the script, as in a re-run, because it's the predictability of family that will be of greatest comfort to you in these uncertain times. Even if you are a sheep with a bad reputation amongst the flock, right or wrong, you can bank on family sticking up for family — if not for you then at least for your kids.

22 Your guardian angel

Golden rule 2: 'Show me you have the time.'
Golden rule 3: 'Show me you have the place.'

There is one person in your life you can truly count on, as you probably have in the past, and who could also be a powerful ally and a real asset in your quest for the care of your kids. She's your guardian angel, better known as your mum. Jane will have a very difficult time discrediting her, especially if she was one of the people handing out advice when Jane herself became a mother. She may also be able to provide some mature and convincing insights into your relationship and her grandchildren.

You see, grandmothers have already graduated from the school of raising children. They have experience beyond our own and are often keen to share this knowledge. Apart from the light a guardian angel can shed on this dark situation, she also has a sacred relationship with your children. Your kids' grandmother would need to have fatal flaws or some serious health problems for Jane to rule her out as an appropriate supervising carer for your kids.

"As a parent, you might see it as a bit of a slap in the face, but agreeing to have a supervisor could remove any reservations a court might have."

As a parent, you might see it as a bit of a slap in the face, but agreeing to have a supervisor could remove any reservations a court might have. Cases these days can take many months before they go to trial or some form of graduated care is ordered. Where interim orders are needed, your guardian angel can be a key to gaining access to your children. If your kids are not of school age, now you're flying solo your guardian angel will be invaluable for all kinds of parental advice you'll need when things aren't all smiles and giggles.

Your guardian angel may also be your greatest confidante. If you were ever in need of your mother's help, it's probably now, and though we're supposed to be all grown up and out the door, most of us are lucky that her door is always open. If Jane has given you the boot, and where you are staying is not ideal, seriously consider or at least discuss a temporary arrangement. Staying with your mum might not seem cool to your mates. It might even drastically restrict your social life. But your kids will be stoked to be close to her, and that should be reason enough. Apart from your kids getting to spend quality time with her, she may be the one person in the world who thinks her son has done no wrong, and this bias may help stabilise your ship while it's under attack.

> "If Jane refuses to leave the kids in your care, your guardian angel can offer the court a real option or at least reduce Jane's fears for their wellbeing."

If Jane refuses to leave the kids in your care, your guardian angel can offer the court a real option or at least reduce Jane's fears for their wellbeing. It may also please a court that paternal grandparents are able to spend quality time with your children during visits or interim care arrangements.

At some stage you may have thought your mum had passed her expiry date, and that the onus was now on you to look after her in her later years. It's funny how wrong we can be sometimes. Now, more than ever, may be the time in your life when your mother is of great influence and support. She may even be prepared to take on the responsibility of being named in a court order, which may prove to be more than just a blessing in disguise.

23 Friends, who needs them anyway?

Golden rule 1: 'You both think you're right.'

They say in life we choose our friends, not our family. But in this situation, nothing could be further from the truth. The longer the relationship with Jane lasted, the more of your friends became 'our' friends. Blood may be thicker than water but your friends, can also separate just like your family. When the salt of those you have chosen to know is put to the test, things rarely taste the same again. This struggle may directly affect the makeup of your family, but the friends you have kept through thick and thin are under no obligation to take your side and support you.

Because this struggle is such a personal one, finding a consensus among your friends is near impossible. Everyone is entitled to their own opinion; some share their views all too willingly while others will reserve their judgment till after the event. Although you may gain an insight into the character of your mates, it's your choice to put them in a difficult situation or right in the middle of a battle. Your mates are not peace-keepers by trade, nor are they soldiers of fortune. They help and need help; they have accepted your faults and have a few of their own. But if you want to remain friends, think about how much you want to involve them. It's not their fault this is happening — that is, unless one of them cut your lunch. Even if some may think they have answers, they may really not want to be involved. These kinds of conversations are seldom good news stories. You're far better off arguing over which team is going to win this weekend than about Jane and kids.

> "The Australian male possesses a unique quality of being there for his mates when the chips are down."

They might already have been through a similar experience. If so, don't be begging for advice; wait for it to be offered. The Australian male possesses a unique quality of being there for his mates when the chips are down. Knowing what and when and where to say something is an art. So be patient, and don't think your mates aren't aware you're hurting or what you might be going through. Beer advice is of no real value; it may sound comforting, but it's unlikely to help you resolve this issue. It's more important that despite half of your world falling down, the other half doesn't. Continuing to do what you usually do with your mates is more important than having a breakdown in front of them. No one likes to see a man crying into his beer, and whether or not they know what to say, chances are their offering won't change your situation.

What you may find if you choose to broach this subject with members of your lodge is that attendance at your beer forums soon dwindles. Keep touch-footy night about the game and not your case or court. There's a good chance other blokes on the team want to forget about their stuff, just for a while. After all, the last thing you need from your mates is for them to pat you on the back and say halfheartedly, 'Everything'll be all right, mate'. If a friend names a good solicitor, then listen up. If others are willing to share practical knowledge gained from experience, then take it on board. It's far better to listen than to pour your heart out in an avalanche of hemotions and man-feelings.

The one thing you'll be sure of before the dust settles is who your real mates are. There are some friends who would rather not be piggy-in-the-middle, and joining them as they sit on the fence will prove difficult. These pork chops are your mutual friends, the ones you met along the way with Jane or the ones who may have once been exclusively yours but are now friends to you both. These friends can be like a deer trapped in your headlights that doesn't know which way to run. They may choose to end growing social speculation and side with either you or Jane, or simply to vanish from sight. The ones who try to remain impartial, or even to broker a peace, often end up resenting the entire situation or are themselves resented. It's a no-win situation for everyone. Involving your mutual friends is like literally dragging a spectator from the stands, handing them a red cape and asking them to join the bullfight.

> "It's far better to listen than to pour your heart out in an avalanche of hemotions and man-feelings."

The rule of thumb here is not to keep your friends out of it but rather, if you value and want to maintain these relationships in the future, to keep it out of your friends' lives. Unfortunately these trusted souls are not the ones to rely on for advice and do not have the power to fix the situation, regardless of any influence they may have over Jane. Friendships are like vases: keep them safe and they may last forever, but overfill them and they will topple and break, sometimes beyond repair, no matter how much superglue you apply. Keep your friends safe and free from harm, and try not to let them see it getting to you either. The ones who withdraw from view are trying to tell you something, but don't think the ones you share things with are your confidants. Your mates are brilliant at being mates, but don't burden them or test their salt with this one. If they are mates and see you drowning, trust they will come to the rescue and throw you a lifeline when and where they see fit.

24 The X factor

Golden rule 1: 'You both think you're right.'

If you still have your hands, chances are you have never handled dynamite. If you are missing both hands, you'll have a good idea how explosive it is. Consider for a moment that Jane is like that volatile substance and needs to be handled with care, more so than you may have used in marriage. Jane is the X factor in your quest for an equitable parenting arrangement. The X in this equation is both a known and an unknown quantity, remember what Huxley said? You will be aware of some of the damage done during your time together, but you also need to be prepared for any amount of blame she is likely to attribute to you. If Jane is renowned for displays of irrational behaviour, emotional outbursts, hostility or dishing out punishment, you are best advised to handle it with extreme care. You may know what to expect but you need to take precautions in case of any potential volatility.

"Despite the dangers, Jane is neither your target nor your enemy. She is simply the mother of your children."

Despite the dangers, Jane is neither your target nor your enemy. She is simply the mother of your children. As much as you might like to rain on her parade, don't. Instead, see the end of your relationship as the end of the fight or disagreement. Put it behind you, but not to bed. If Jane chooses to go to war, then make sure your actions are not reactions to her behaviour. You are now independent yet in a strange way still dependent. You're not a yo-yo, but if you choose to see her as the enemy there is a good chance you will feel like you have been round the world and over the falls. Whatever she does, says, writes, states, proclaims or thinks is something to observe, like bird watching, not something to react to impulsively. The more you react to her, whatever it may be about this time, the greater the unknown factors become. If you push Jane too far, there could be no return from such a place, and if you're still hoping to see the kids, hope may be all you'll have left to hang on to. Arguments or disagreements will only lead you astray and be used to portray you as less than agreeable in this situation. In the afterlife with Jane you don't need to be the bigger man, just a more patient and gentle man.

Understand that Jane will always harbour feelings for you, good, bad or indifferent, though it may be best to never inquire about them. Kids aren't made of glue, and using them to repair your relationship is a fundamentally flawed idea. You may be better off resigning yourself to the reality that if it wasn't broken you wouldn't need to fix it. But somehow, in this afterlife with Jane, you will need to rebuild the relationship or the unknowns in your future may include your kids, your happiness and maybe even your sanity.

A good idea is to make this new relationship as simple as possible. You might want it to run like clockwork, but women have always been known to change their minds, so why would your Jane be an exception? At best, some of her actions will be pedestrian and about as comforting as public transport. Regardless you need to be as precise as a Swiss clock at all times to reduce the chances of unknown factors from arising.

Someone once wrote that men and women come from different planets, and we probably do. Understanding the lore of the jungle is a key to reducing the unknown X factors of Jane. Though the relationship you now have with her may at times seem to be completely off this planet, you will have to manage it and tolerate her even more than you may have in marriage. No matter how far she shoots for the stars of bad behaviour, you must remember to handle her with care at all times. In many ways it is an exercise in middle management, where you need to manage all factors, known and unknown, or she is likely to stand between you and your kids. Yes, you will have to work at it harder than you ever have and handle any potentially explosive situation with extreme care. But by doing so you will reduce the impact of the X factor, increasing both the predictability of the future and, best of all, the time you'll spend with your children.

"Understanding the lore of the jungle is a key to reducing the unknown X factors of Jane."

25 The out-laws

Golden rule 1: 'You both think you're right.'

Your out-laws, who were once your in-laws, now rule the dark side of your life. Whether they are giving you their two cents worth or presenting affidavits to the court, at least you have a good idea who Jane's army of the dead includes. Though you may have separated from her, for some reason the out-laws are a little harder to excommunicate.. When it comes to the care of your children, it's not really their business, but you're bound to hear it all the same. Luckily the courts recognise that the dispute is a parental one, between you and Jane, and despite their claims or interference their opinions are little more than that.

That said, there's a matter that's a little more complex called life, which somehow allows this band of not so merry men and women to think they are welcome at the table of opinion years after the deal has been cancelled. 'Why?' is the cry of single fathers across the land. Unfortunately they are part of your children's family; it's there in the fine print. So be prepared to turn the other cheek to their unwanted abuse.

"There's a matter that's a little more complex called life, which somehow allows this band of not so merry men and women to think they are welcome at the table of opinion years after the deal has been cancelled."

The out-laws are normally fronted by the Dragon, commonly known as the ex-mother-in-law. Never confront the Dragon without a proven strategy. They are normally one eyed and to be avoided or at least kept beyond reach and shouting distance. The Henchmen, or former brothers-in-law, who may have once sat at the table of mates, may or may not be an evil threat and can often be bribed with man-drink. However, if things do get ugly with Jane, or you try to slay the Dragon, be ready to make a run for it. An assault charge stemming from an altercation on Jane's front lawn isn't a good look in court and may also trigger an AVO or DVO. Plus you can bet such an incident will be brought up by the dark side in proceedings for the care of your kids. If confronted by an out-law, just run away, run away and you'll live to see your kids another day.

The Ugly Sisters often like to bring the bling. You'll likely get the stare of death more often than not from these characters, but remember, they're the ones who have to look at themselves in the mirror every morning. Still, you may need to communicate through them if the lines are down with Jane, perhaps to arrange suitable times and places to pick up your kids. The Demons, Jane's aunties, can be quite daunting and may approach the battleground with a small platoon of their own. Again, you need to identity which evil spirit has the influence over Jane and hope that something you got her for Christmas one year was a winner.

The Demons of Jane may have hit-men of their own, your ex-uncles. Again, these brokers outside the feminine powerbase can be somewhat sympathetic to your cause, especially if they have rowed a similar boat to yours. If they have travelled the track you now tread, their knowledge of its potholes and pitfalls, not to mention a few out-law family secrets, could be worth knowing.

Judgement from above is certain to come from the Ghosts of Jane's grandparents. Whether this proves to be a blessing or a curse on your life will depend on how well you have nurtured these relationships over the years. But remember, they too are part of your children's 'family' and you should never give them a serve or any ammunition.

And yes there is one other, unofficial, over-opinionated class: the soldiers of dread. These mindless mobs are Jane's friends and may have been waiting for years to sink the boot in. Though some may have shared a beer with you in the past, it is guaranteed that few will share one with you in the future. Try not to draw these troops into your confidence, as inevitably anything said to them will be served up to Jane like Chinese takeaway.

> "Dealing with these relationships is really unwarranted, but it's necessary if you are to set a good example as an unbiased parent."

Dealing with these relationships is really unwarranted, but it's necessary if you are to set a good example as an unbiased parent. You need to have a clean score sheet heading into court, so don't give them anything that could be developed into a screenplay that's critical of you. If you can maintain a civil dialogue, do so, but do so with caution. It's unlikely you'll ever sway their opinion, and bagging Jane, or taking them on, is only going to create more enemies. Just be careful what you share with these people. They are Jane's family, whether you like them or not.

26 Enter the Dragon

Golden rule 1: 'You both think you're right.'

There may have been times when, confronted by your fire-breathing, bad-tempered, older than the hills dragon of a mother-in-law, you wished you were blessed with Bruce Lee's moves. But those nightmares could be nothing if Jane decides to let this beast off the chain now. If she does, you may be able to put some daylight between you and her over the first couple of hundred metres or so, but dragons never give up, or change their minds. And when it comes to the subject of 'the one who broke my daughter's heart', the title of 'home wrecker' will be carved in stone under your name.

The Dragon is not your friend, which is often a blessing in disguise, but in the land of the afterlife you now share with Jane, the Dragon is to be avoided like the plague. The less you have to do with this one-eyed, scaly old reptile the better off you'll be. Please Do Not Feed the Dragon, ever! Dragons are known to do one of two things if given a serve. They may choose to digest it only to regurgitate it at a later date in the presence of Jane or a court, when you can bet the winged lizard will put on a B-grade acting show. But the preferred option of the Dragon is to breathe fire, and apart from the bad breath she will set you ablaze. Simply trying to converse or reason with the Dragon can be dangerous, even life threatening.

> "The Dragon will always believe Jane, who walks on water."

So stop entertaining the idea that you can negotiate with such a beast. You can't. The Dragon will always believe Jane, who walks on water, has only ever loved and supported you and has never done you wrong. You can try suiting up in your best armour, polish it all night if you want, but no matter how narcissistic it is the Dragon won't be distracted by its own reflection. If you are confronted and cornered by this mother-in-law of all creatures, don't attack. Hold your ground, but do not engage the Dragon or all hell could break loose. There are no points to be won in a slinging match on the footpath or over the phone. Apart from these battles being unwinnable, they are only going to end up recorded in her and Jane's affidavits.

Reason is of no interest to her either. The Dragon isn't about to change sides or advocate for your cause, certainly not while Jane is withholding the kids from you. At best, you are advised to let dragons be. Don't think they sleep with their one eye closed either. Dragons see all and think they know all too. They often claim to be authoritative and don't mind saying so. This is where their weakness lies, when their vulnerable underbelly is exposed, especially when Jane's dirty washing is aired. But best leave your sword in its sheath and leave the slaying to your solicitor. If at any time during your quest the Dragon crosses your path, just wave politely as you head for the hills. Don't feed it or reason with it, bribe it or bait it, because dragons breathe fire and you'll only get burned.

27 Madonna and your kids

Golden rule 1: 'You both think you're right.'

The image of the Madonna and Child is an iconic representation of motherhood. All the great thinkers, from Darwin to Freud to Piaget and the rest of them, have recognised the significant, if not inseparable, bond that exists between a mother and her child. Unfortunately for fathers today, the courts recognise this too. Give a bloke some credit: it is our wrigglers that give life to the egg. But it's women who grow them, and then remind us of the torture of childbirth and the eternal debt we owe them. The problem is that although they give us children, these days they are also prone to taking them away.

It's critical that you understand this early on: that it really is Mt Everest that rises before you. As ominous as this may sound, if you stage your journey and pace yourself, reaching the summit of resolution may not require breathing apparatus. Adopt this biological understanding and Jane, who will also need to agree to some terms and conditions, may prove to be a lesser evil than expected.

Honour the mother, even if she did kick you out on the street, because your kids more than likely do. Perhaps you have done this already, or had it done to you, but what you need to do is to separate the wife from the mother. A mother is a guardian of her children. The problem is she may be guarding her children from *you*.

> "Honour the mother, even if she did kick you out on the street, because your kids more than likely do."

Respecting her as a mother is usually possible, regardless of how sour the relationship has become. Acknowledging something simple like the kids' good health may just catch her off guard and score you a point against the run of play. The bond that exists between your kids and their mum is precious, whether or not you think she's pulling her weight. Unfortunately, the strength of this relationship may create thoughts in her head like 'I'm not going to give up my kid(s) without a fight'. Yes, it's a natural instinct of mothers to be more than reluctant to let their children go. But if you recognise rather than ignore this fundamental bond between Madonna and her children, you'll realise it's about not disturbing the sleeping lion than it is about big game hunting.

Even if you are the most reasonable bloke on the planet, you're almost guaranteed to experience some form of resistance from Jane. Yes, they are your kids too, but the lore of the jungle and of nature both rule over her house of feminine logic. Lucky for you, the law of Australia is the one you are both required to observe.

> "Even if you are the most reasonable bloke on the planet, you're almost guaranteed to experience some form of resistance from Jane."

The younger your children, the more reluctant Jane will be to let them go. It's true, women can have successful careers and bear the responsibility of raising children on their own, but so can men. Luckily, the court also recognises the important role a father plays in the emotional, social, physical, cognitive and psychological development of a child, whether Jane does or not.

To re-enter the land of your children you must first get past Jane the gatekeeper. Don't be concerned with trolls under bridges or gruff billygoats. She who guards the gate to the Promised Land can easily become aggressive if threatened. Although she might struggle to recognise your role as a father, just remember that, apart from the dinner service she got for her twenty-first, the kids are her most prized possession. Approach the entrance with caution and in a non-threatening manner. The gentler you are with Jane, the less she will resist your requests and the greater will be your chance of seeing your kids. The more you agitate, push and poke her, the longer the gate may remain locked.

The language you use, the baits you choose not to take, and an underlying patience that comes from an awareness of what you're playing for, will get results. It makes sense that the less you fight, the more peace you will have. But don't expect the keys to the kingdom in an instant. Your idea of what would be just and fair, and of the benefits of a father's care and influence, will be different from hers. When you begin to give thanks to the Madonna and honour her role as a mother, will you'll start to regain some ground in the land of your kids.

28 Emotional investments

Golden rule 1: 'You both think you're right.'

The most destructive investment you can make when seeking to regain a foothold in your children's life is an emotional one. This might seem a perplexing statement given this is the better part of your family you're fighting for, but it's not complicated. The legal process is a very conditional one, with rules and laws governing and guiding each step. The law does not make allowances for or rule on emotions, however. The man-feelings or hemotions you may experience on this journey can take you from the top of Everest to the bottom of the deep blue sea, but at no time can you allow them to dictate your actions or rule your behaviour.

There will be times when you feel great pain and there will be other times when you feel nothing. But feelings will do nothing to help you achieve a good outcome. Hemotions can be deceptive, and this task may evoke some you have never experienced before, but allowing these guys to be the back-seat driver of your mind is fraught with danger. Everybody hurts, but a judge won't rule on this alone. Calling upon hemotions to fuel your efforts is like throwing petrol on a fire; your case is likely to go up in smoke.

> "Wearing your heart on your sleeve is only going to get it dirty, caught on something or torn open altogether."

Jumping on the phone, texting or tweeting threats to Jane won't help your cause either. It will simply strengthen her case. You might think it is impossible to separate your man-feelings from your actions, but if you choose not to, then separation is what you may end up experiencing permanently. Rather than using your hemotions, sort them out. A shrink may prescribe something for your emotional pain but it won't necessarily fix it. A sound investment may be a counsellor, someone you can work with to maintain a healthy perspective no matter how much pain the current situation causes you. Or you join a mens group, after all blokes know all too well that shed happens.

Wearing your heart on your sleeve is only going to get it dirty, caught on something or torn open altogether. Standing there like a stunned mullet or a deer in the headlights isn't helpful either. Going on a hemotional spending spree will inevitably leave you bankrupt. To place all your savings on a horse called hope is a massive gamble and one that is unlikely to pay off. If the man-feelings begin to boil over it's worth sharing them with someone who can help you get them under control, rather than medicating and numbing the pain they are causing. The more you keep these unwanted allies in the barracks, the more you'll have to spend on your kids in the future.

29 Shop around

Golden rule 2: 'Show me you have the time.'
Golden rule 3: 'Show me you have the place.'

One of the great advantages Jane may have over you, apart from having the kids and being their mother, is that women like to shop. Shopping around is something you need to do if you're going to find a solicitor who fits your needs. You'll discover a plenitude of solicitors on the web and in the phonebook. There are new ones and experienced ones, expensive ones and very expensive ones. Some are more argumentative than others, and some are more agreeable than most. They come in all shapes and sizes and are found throughout the land. Which one you choose to represent you depends on how much time and effort you're willing to invest.

Referrals are handy. In this line of work, if their own result was unfavourable, former clients will be reluctant to recommend their solicitor to others. Cost will be a major factor in your choice. Some say the closer to town, and the higher up you go in the lift, the more it's going to cost you. Many offer a free initial consultation. It may be true that those who can pick and choose their cases do, but you owe it to yourself and your children to listen to more than one opinion. Being able to get your story across without sounding like a broken record or bursting into tears is very important. The more time you allow them to talk during the consultation, the more you're going to know whether they are on your wavelength.

"Male or female, it doesn't matter and probably never will; after all it's not a dancing competition."

Some say if you start at the very top and plead your case to the best, then you will be limiting the quality of representation available to Jane. A solicitor can't take on her case if they heard your story first. This is a valid consideration, but you may end up spending a truckload of money and the rest of your natural life warming up rather than in the game. Male or female, it doesn't matter and probably never will; after all it's not a dancing competition. Someone who fits your bill is as important as whether or not you are able to foot their bill. What you're looking for is as much experience as you can afford, not simply in building cases or appearances before a judge, but in negotiating agreements and care arrangements. Asking them about the outcomes of similar cases they have handled may help you with your final selection. Ultimately, you will need to make a choice, and if you have spent the time and invested the energy in telling your story to at least a couple of legal firms, hopefully you'll find one that's right for you.

WELCOME TO THE JUNGLE

30 Your case or a night at the movies

Golden rule 1: 'You both think you're right.'
Golden rule 2: 'Show me you have the time.'
Golden rule 3: 'Show me you have the place.'

In a sense your case is like a movie; just make sure it's worth the cost of admission. What genre of flick it turns out to be is completely up to you. Ultimately it will be written and directed by you, and no doubt star you. How long it screens in court is not a sign of success or popularity. If it does run longer than a Kevin Costner movie marathon, you're probably going to see a big blowout in production costs. It might be mainly a one-man show and enough to make any bloke a little self-conscious, but that's not an excuse to start acting like a movie star. Hopefully it's a story of a man who has shown great patience, dedication and consideration, none of which require any special effects.

If your case is rated R and looks destined to be compared to a horror classic, you'll probably end up having nightmares. Even if you believe Jane is acting like a poltergeist, it doesn't mean you should be adding to the theatrics. Engaging in behaviour that children should not view, or passing off conflict as entertainment, isn't going to rate real well. If your case contains scenes that might be out-takes from a kung fu film, then you'll probably go home empty handed rather than with an Oscar. Dramas don't draw much attention from the audience either, and if your cast includes thousands, your case may end up being more epic than you imagined. Any B-grade acting should not be blamed on the script, so it's best to remember your lines. There's obviously some level of mystery to the story, but the less that appears, the more creditable your performance will be.

> "If your case is rated R and looks destined to be compared to a horror classic, you'll probably end up having nightmares."

Worse still, your case could be seen as comical, full of slapstick routines emphasising the stupidity of your actions. It's not that you'll ever be seen as the laughing stock of the court, but acting the clown, or being portrayed as one by your biggest critic, could cast serious doubt on your competence as a parent. Acting like an action hero or some sort of superhero won't win you many points either. Overacting tends to suggest dishonesty. Let the truth be the star, supported by facts and detailed records. The one genre you should avoid at all cost is science fiction. Apart from the big increase in budget needed to create such illusions, the chances that your intergalactic fairytale will be given credit are slim.

What you are looking to produce is not going to come out of a Hollywood studio. Rather, you should stick to the documentary format. Presenting the facts and figures and providing detailed observations is what your picture should focus on, rather than cheap stunts. Sadly it's not a love story with a happy ending. Sure, it began with romantic scenes, but a wicked twist and a bit of tragedy guaranteed an ending that is far from predictable. Documentaries are usually produced on a low budget and rarely include a cast of thousands. The best ones are painstakingly accurate in their portrayal of events and allow an audience to draw considered conclusions rather than being forced to watch a mystery. In court the less drama the better. The less you rely on special effects, the more plausible your narrative will appear. After all, you're not being nominated for an acting award. Hopefully, the critics will agree in due course that there is merit in your portrayal of a father who wants to parent his children.

"The less you rely on special effects, the more plausible your narrative will appear. After all, you're not being nominated for an acting award."

31 No 100% guarantee

Golden rule 1: 'You both think you're right.'
Golden rule 2: 'Show me you have the time.'
Golden rule 3: 'Show me you have the place.'

These days all the road signs point towards the benefits of a shared care arrangement for your children, whether or not Jane agrees. But court is no guarantee of an equitable shared care outcome at the end of this yellow brick road. Despite the recommendations of solicitors and mediators, and the setting up of a parenting order to that effect, Jane might still not play ball. The fact is there are many ifs and buts that may need answering to determine what's best for your children.

Though you may be concerned about Jane's unwillingness to share, the court will not rule on this alone. What the court will need to create a shared care parenting order is for both parents to communicate effectively and have the capacity, now and into the foreseeable future, to maintain that order. Inevitably, the more agreeable, patient, tolerant and flexible you are, the more favourably the court will view a shared parenting agreement.

Whether your case has landed in the Family Court or Federal Magistrates (Circuit) Court of Australia, you can be sure that much consideration will be given to all material presented before the court. The court gives no guarantee of an equitable outcome. Rather, it is required to consider whether spending equal time with both parents is in the best interests of the children and practical to do so. Considerations aren't guarantees; they are a means of examination and not a promise or obligation. The court will also consider the benefit to your children of developing and maintaining a meaningful relationship with both their parents.

> "Considerations aren't guarantees; they are a means of examination and not a promise or obligation."

At all times the court must consider the children's need to be protected from physical and psychological harm, neglect abuse, domestic and family violence. While every consideration is given to permitting equal access to both parents, sadly some parents are judged not to offer an acceptable environment or role model for children. So again, the need to pursue this process in a consistently civil, non-aggressive and non-threatening manner is essential if the court is to be convinced that you pose no foreseeable risk to your child's physical and mental health.

If for some reason the court decides against making an order for the shared care of your children, then there is a second-chance draw, or what the law calls substantial or 'significant time'. This recognises the fact that although your children do not live with you, or you are not named as the primary carer, you are still their father. So, where practical, your children should have the opportunity to spend time with you during the week and on weekends, holidays and other significant days or events. A significant gain for single dads is that, where a shared care order may not have been seen as viable, spending significant time ensures that fathers aren't necessarily cast in the role of 'weekend dads'.

> "But what you can be guaranteed of as a father is that the court is going to consider what's best for your children and that may not necessarily include how Jane has been acting."

Court is a lot more practical than you might think. Yes, there are no guarantees of a shared care arrangement, but you can be sure that the court promptly gets down to business. In considering the practicalities of a parenting order, it will examine contributing factors such as the distance between parents' residences, the capacity of both parties to maintain any order, the ability of both parties to communicate and the impact the agreement will have on the kids and any other matter the court wishes to consider. There are no guarantees of a shared care arrangement, even if your case does end up in court. But what you can be guaranteed of as a father is that the court is going to consider what's best for your children and that may not necessarily include how Jane has been acting. If your case ticks the right boxes, and after considering the potential effects of the order on your children, including the proximity and appropriateness of the home environments, there exists a chance, even if not a 100% guarantee, that you may achieve an equitable share in a parenting order for your kids.

32 The simple truth

Golden rule 1: 'You both think you're right.'

In matters and situations like these, emotions can run wild and become uncontrollable. Your hemotions can lead you astray and send you off in the wrong direction like a disoriented tourist. It pays to pack light for the journey, and the more man-feelings you leave behind before embarking, the sooner you will reach your destination. Although Australian men don't do a great trade in such commodities, hemotions can surface at the most inopportune times. They are complex chemical reactions that are as practical as looking for a sharp object in the dark. Even when you do discover them, you can end up losing a digit, or even a limb.

"Although simple, the truth is of far greater consequence than any hemotion-driven recollection of an event."

The truth should be as clear as a pool of fresh water. It's transparent, doesn't claim to be anything it's not and is essential in forming the basis of any simple solution. Hemotions don't make you lie; they do, however, muddy the waters. The truth is what your case needs to be made of, rather than emotional responses, accusations and embellishments. The simple truth is, and should always be, easy to read and understand. It's not likely to be complex either. The truth relies on facts like, who was involved, what occurred and when and the whereabouts events took place.

Although simple, the truth is of far greater consequence than any hemotion-driven recollection of an event. It is also really all your solicitor, the mediator or the judge is interested in hearing. It's that simple. How you felt is not as important as what actually happened and how the events unfolded. Saying that Jane is 'crazy' is just a perspective and 'is trying to get back at you' is only a motive. But neither is the truth. That's just a judgement and how she made you feel. This isn't the role you need to play in this. You're there simply to state the facts. Everyone hurts (and everyone knows that), but not everyone tells the truth. Lies are driven by emotions and normally become all too evident during proceedings.

If the truth is still difficult to see, look more closely, as it's often in the detail. Broad, sweeping assumptions and statements are driven by hemotion and tend to generalise rather than being specific. The simple truth is easy to describe, define and detail. The truth fits together like a jigsaw to create a picture, rather than being an image created with one giant stroke of the brush. Your story doesn't need to be 'picture perfect'. What's required is a clear recollection of events and actions, rather than theories of conspiracy and mistrust.

"Sticking to the simple truth in every situation and communication will prevent the thunder clouds from gathering and raining on your parade."

The simple truth is you want to parent your kids, so why introduce anything else into the equation? Hemotions are like uninvited guests and will only wreck the place. Communicating anything but the simple truth to Jane or a court is only going to create more conflict and delay a resolution. Allowing your hemotions to dictate your behaviour will present badly for you and end up in her paperwork. Keeping your man-feelings at home, out of sight, out of mind and out of your case is what's best for your kids. Sticking to the simple truth in every situation and communication will prevent the thunder clouds from gathering and raining on your parade.

33 Wish you were here

Golden rule 2: 'Show me you have the time.'
Golden rule 3: 'Show me you have the place.'

Lament in the single father's dictionary is defined as a man who has lost contact with his kids. The saying 'You don't know what you have till you lose it' often resonates with those going through separation and divorce. Only after winning a grand final can you know the true cost of losing one. In this game you now find yourself in, Jane may change her colours, move the goalposts and bend the rules whenever it suits. You may have been kicked like a lazy dog and turfed out of your castle, but you can only lament for so long. You have the choice of either licking your wounds and getting back up or rolling over and playing dead.

"Time's the only medicine you need to heal, but perhaps you'll require a lot of it."

A good indication the lamenting has truly set in is when the bottom of your beer glass begins to occupy your attention. Your mates around the table are probably waiting for the next round and are likely to avoid the topic as much as they avoid their wives. These guys will be aware of your suffering and may know that things are going to rack and ruin, but really these blokes are your mates, not counsellors. The local watering hole is not the best place to be seen or heard discussing your plight. Don't confuse their offers to take you down to the pub for genuine interest in your problems. It may be just a simple act of kindness to help take your mind off things and give you a break from your thoughts.

Time's the only medicine you need to heal, but perhaps you'll require a lot of it. You need time to process things, to forgive people for their actions, to build a new life and home. Having to do these things can be a good thing. The truth is, although things are different, that can be a blessing in disguise. Every bloke, although a mirror of perfection, can use the time to tune up in a number of areas.

How you use the time you might have had with your kids will partly depend on whether you choose to see the beer glass as half full or whether you see the glass at all. Give up smoking while no one's around, go to the gym or take up a hobby. Work on yourself and get your house in order. Your home is not simply the place where you live; it's also the life you lead and the people in it. If you are between places or still in makeshift accommodation that is inappropriate for children, then all is not lost. Taking them to visit your guardian angel, or their aunts or uncles might be okay with Jane. Even if she thinks you're incompetent, visiting family is often an acceptable option. You would not be the first father to think the shoe should be on the other foot, but your mum is also a mum, and can provide valuable parental advice, especially if your kids are young. She's also a grandmother and would probably love to spend time with her grandchildren. Jane may agree that family occasions like birthdays or religious events are important for your children to attend. You might wish they were with you more often, but when things are up in the air and undecided, maintaining contact with them can be a huge achievement.

The other house you need to get in order is your case. You don't need to watch a mini-series of forensic mysteries or undertake a private detective's course; you just need to be diligent. Often the best way for a man to do something about his lament is to apply himself to the task at hand. Getting to work and dealing with your situation before it becomes a saga is an important part of parenting. The sooner you pick yourself up and dust yourself off, the happier your children will be. Grit your teeth, grin and bear it, put your nose to the grindstone and your back to the wall. There might be a mountain you need to climb, but that's better than trying to get around it. If Jane is the disagreeable type, then reaching the summit may require a great deal of patience and effort. But the sooner you begin to work on rebuilding yourself and creating a place for your kids, the sooner your life will shift from lament into top gear.

"The other house you need to get in order is your case. You don't need to watch a mini-series of forensic mysteries or undertake a private detective's course; you just need to be diligent."

34 Winners and losers

Golden rule 1: 'You both think you're right.'

In the tug of war that has erupted over the kids, and the many lesser battles that will occur, there is unlikely to be a winner and will most likely be three losers. There are three sides to this story, not two as most parents think, whether or not they are acting like adults. In fact adults play second fiddle in this song and dance, regardless of who ends up footing the bill. The court is no place to play tennis, and judges are not umpires. They are not so much concerned with on-field behaviour as they are for the welfare of the third party involved, and they will assign an independent solicitor for them if required.

"Court is not a holiday destination. It's the last resort when all reasonable attempts at resolution have failed."

The children, your kids, are the piggies in the middle. These fleet-footed centres of attention are the ones who will end up winners or losers from all this kerfuffle. Parents are simply the ones who will pay for the fallout, however it plays out over the years to come in the lives of their children and in ways not yet imagined. From misdirected emotions to antisocial and violent behaviour, your actions in this fight will be seen, judged and learned by your children. It's true, the more we fight the more we hurt the ones we love the most, even if they aren't the ones we are arguing with.

Inevitably, second place in this three-horse race is the best you can hope for. You may end up sharing pole position on the grid in your children's lives, but the carnage caused in qualifying won't be celebrated with a victory lap, or by your kids. Everyone in your family will undergo a change. Your kids may end up living in two homes or not seeing their father infrequently or not at all. You may have escaped Jane's cooking, but your kids may not enjoy any respite till week's end. Kids have a right to be happy. It's a parent's responsibility to ensure this, even if you are staging your own personal Vietnam.

Though essentially a place of resolution, the court can be a bit like a boxing match. They say that it's always best to end the fight in the ring rather than let the judges decide. Many who preside over these matters may agree. Judges aren't there to award gold medals or crown a new champion. Their role is to make a decision for the benefit of your children, based on the information supplied and what they can salvage from the remains of your once loving relationship. A barrister once remarked that 'a good decision is a fair decision and a fair decision is a considered one'. The idea behind this game is to knock the argument on the head rather than Jane. Whether it's a slanging match on the footpath or a slinging match in the courts, the more you fight the more likely it is that the judge will make the decisions, in accordance with the law, in the best interest of your children.

Court is not a holiday destination. It's the last resort when all reasonable attempts at resolution have failed. Even then opportunities for your counsel to strike a deal with Jane's legal representatives will be encouraged to avoid the court having to make the final decision. If your situation is extreme, however, and all that waving of olive branches has you feeling like a shrub, and you haven't seen the kids for months, maybe it's the court you need to put your faith in. If Jane is brought kicking and screaming to court, you may have won a small battle in the process.

> "In a sense, your presence in court is a plea for help and in effect you are placing the care of your children in the hands of the judge."

In a sense, your presence in court is a plea for help and in effect you are placing the care of your children in the hands of the judge. So, if all deals are off and the gloves are on, take a deep breath and be prepared to accept the court's decision. For one or a hundred reasons things might not seem fair as they are currently, but know that when the bell tolls there is likely to be only one winner. It may not be you, but it won't be Jane either. A fair decision by the court is a good result, and one that is ultimately best for your kids.

35 Running the risk

Golden rule 1: 'You both think you're right.'

Government swears by it, good business evaluates it, the reckless fly in the face of it and the courts practise it. Risk aversion is a major force to be reckoned with when it comes to the care of your kids. The more you practise it, the more peaceful your jungle will be. What does 'risk aversion' really mean? If it was a road sign it would read: 'Avoid at All Cost'. Perhaps the expression 'Live to fight another day' sheds some light on this conservative term. Or, if you need another, how about 'Stay out of trouble's way'. Trouble, in matters of the heart and your family, can take many different forms.

What parent would willingly teach their kid to argue? Someone who enjoys being yelled at? The overwhelming majority of the unofficial parenting association of Australia would agree that teaching your children bad habits will inevitably come back to haunt you. The amount of mud-slinging with the Jane in your relationship, and how much your kids were witness to it, will become evident both in your case and your children's lives.

One thing you will learn over the course of these trials and tribulations is that there's not much you can do about the past, apart from reconciling with it. But, and it's a big but, it starts as soon as you stop repeating it. Before your conversation with Jane heads south, take action to avoid it by applying a little risk aversion. It's not like sun tan lotion. All you need do is simply walk away and leave the argument for today.

Avoiding confrontation, and demonstrating tolerance and patience with Jane in the afterlife, will show a judge or mediator that you are risk averse. The less confrontational you are, the greater your chances will be of landing a shared care arrangement. There are of course other factors that will determine this, but being a risk-adverse individual won't hurt your chances. How Jane behaves is up to her. You probably couldn't control it in your relationship and you have little influence now. If you don't participate in an argument, Jane's actions will simply reflect her bad behaviour. If she is unwilling to share or at least consider your parenting suggestions and wishes, allow this to define her, not you.

You can bet that the courts will apply the required amount of risk aversion to your case from start to finish and at all times during it. Whatever orders or arrangements are handed down, you can guarantee they will have 'risk aversion' stencilled into every line. Don't take it personally, because the courts won't. They *will* attempt to minimise any violence or abuse in the lives of your kids, and that's something to be grateful about. Choose confrontation as a means to finding a solution and you could be running the risk of losing a place in your children's futures. Begin applying some risk aversion in the management of your afterlife with Jane and you could find your children have a place in your life a lot sooner than you imagined.

36 Haunted by the past

Golden rule 2: 'Show me you have the time.'
Golden rule 3: 'Show me you have the place.'

Life is about growing up, getting on, looking up and moving on — or at least that's what they say. Making progress is all about looking forward, not back. Yet in this situation, the opportunity to build some momentum in your life is not simple or easy to achieve. The uncertainty that surrounds your relationship with your children makes moving on difficult, but getting on with the rest of your life is important if things are going to start looking up. Your case for being an active parent may feel like it weighs as much as Santa's sack on Christmas Eve, but it's a weight you must shoulder if you are to begin moving onwards and, hopefully, upwards. In this sack is the weight of your past, so until your parenting issues are resolved it's not a good idea to drop your bundle and leave it halfway to nowhere and lying around.

The weight of your situation may be back-breaking at times, but it's your baggage. Although it is important for your children's future to state your case for the future, you can bet the past will also figure heavily. Whether you're prepared to look at what's happened honestly is up to you. Skeletons in your closet that you thought were safely tucked away could easily make a reappearance in Jane's paperwork. Indiscretions of the past, no matter how old, may be raised from the dead, but it's the more likely that recent history will occupy her mind, and described in surprising detail.

Unfortunately a break-up does not wipe the slate clean, and cases can end up looking more like scorecards of separation than plans for the future. In this kind of situation, you become haunted by the past and may end up being judged in retrospect on its indiscretions. There's nothing you can do to rewrite history, but to forget it ever existed could prove fatal to your cause. It is important, no matter how painful it may seem, to dive to the bottom of your Santa's sack and at least review your past. Your version of events is just as relevant as Jane's account. Attributing blame is not as important as taking responsibly. Conveniently overlooking, and failing to inform your counsel of, an event or action you're not real proud of is a big no-no. Your solicitor is not there to judge you, but they do need to know, at least from your perspective, what went on, because you can bet the worst of your behaviour will be tabled by Jane.

How you treated Jane in the past will be seen as a reflection of how you may treat people in the future. So if you do have remorse for some of the less savoury things you're done, it's a good idea to note lessons learned in your affidavits, demonstrating change is not as difficult as it may seem. Golden rules 2 and 3 can help you to move on and design a better world for yourself and your children. We are yet to develop the technology to change the past or correct our mistakes and prevent future regrets. You cannot undo what's been done, but the past presents you with two options. You can either allow it to haunt you for the rest of your life, or you can choose to learn from it and grow up, get on, look up and move on.

FIND THE MIDDLE GROUND

37 For argument's sake

Golden rule 1: 'You both think you're right.'

Fathers are like lasagna, layered with hemotions and man-feelings. Exploration of the sedimentary layers of a man's emotional landscape is rare in most cases, but if you're after an expedient way to drill to the core, then nothing cuts to the bone like losing your kids. Too many marriages these days end in divorce or separation. It's more like: till divorce do we part. The lore of nature demands that children outlive their parents, and for any bloke looking forward to enjoying his later years, having the kids around is going to be essential if they are to experience the joys of being a grandfather.

On the surface, not much bothers us. But the deeper you cut, the more embedded hemotions become. Hemotions don't emanate from the logical part of a man's brain. They may not originate from the brain at all. But they alone have the power to revert a man to a primate state. Being blind to man-feelings is as useful as having a limb amputated. If not watched, hemotions can run wilder than the horses in your top paddock. If not kept under control, they will rule over each thought, gate-crash the party and barge their way into every conversation. If not kept in check, you can guarantee that hemotions will stir up the idiot in any man.

> "Hemotions don't emanate from the logical part of a man's brain. They may not originate from the brain at all."

Worst of all, hemotions are combustible —highly combustible. The deeper down you drill, the more volatile they become. Scientists say that these compounds are unstable, unpredictable and dangerous to anyone who comes in close contact with them. What's worse is that the possibility of losing your kids is enough to arouse such hemotions as to cause others to perceive you as a danger to them. But many men who have allowed their feelings to drive them straight over the cliff of sanity have paid the ultimate price of losing the opportunity to parent their children. Arguments are fuelled by hemotions and can explode like volcanoes when summoned from the depths of a man's being. In the molten heart of men are feelings that make us say things that don't help our cause. Assure Jane you're a capable parent or you may fuel actions that can be irreversible. It doesn't matter how well men might manage to repair things; in one way or another, the damage that's been done is usually still evident.

But there are some man-feelings that don't lend themselves to wanton destruction. They probably used to be on display to Jane, and children are especially susceptible to them. As blokes we dare not mention the word. But any father without his children needs, not to turn up the heat of his emotional barbecue, but to perch himself in the shade of this four-lettered word called *love.*

> "Love your kids, even if they aren't with you. Love Jane, even if you don't anymore, just for argument's sake."

Love your kids, even if they aren't with you. Love Jane, even if you don't anymore, just for argument's sake. But most of all, take the time to find some for you. It's best for all if you find the switch to the furnace in you and turn it down. Of course it's easier said than done, but there's nothing easy about any of these circumstances. The bitter taste of disappointment that stems from regret will do more than just leave a bad taste in your mouth. It may literally ruin your whole day — and night, and the next day and the next night, for years and years to come. Choose to love, even if perhaps not quite the same as before, because fuelling up on hemotion will only end up exploding in your face, and that's definitely not a good look, especially to your kids.

38 Best-case scenario

Golden rule 1: 'You both think you're right.'
Golden rule 2: 'Show me you have the time.'
Golden rule 3: 'Show me you have the place.'

Hoping Jane drops off the face of the Earth may be a soothing thought during these troubled times, but it's not the best-case scenario. Having a Jane who is agreeable and civil is best, because kids need a good mum as much as they need a good dad — equity is everything. If truth be known, the kids would probably like things to go back to the way they were. But the reality is we can't rewind time, and this is not something you can get them for Christmas. How you and Jane think things should change now will more than likely be different, though it's helpful if you're both at least on the same page. If a court is forced to decide what's best for your kids, you can guarantee it will be different from either your or Jane's preferred solution.

"The court, in all cases, would prefer that parents come to their own arrangements, and sometimes the fear of the court's consequence is enough to turn the most stubborn parent around."

It's time to be honest, not right. What's best for you may be best for the kids, but it's unlikely to be what's best for Jane, no matter how much rocket science you apply. Neither will it be the blueprint from which the court will try to find an equitable solution. So before deciding exactly what it is you want for your kids and announcing how, when and where you will be available for them, take a good hard look in the mirror. Consider how this time and place will fit into their world, and how it might also sit in Jane's. Now take one last look and see just how practical your plan is. Because the decision the court hands down will be as simple and achievable as it can be, given its understanding of everyone's situation.

What your kids need is continuity after this speed bump in their early lives; it need not be any more than that, but this is completely dependent on how much you and Jane can agree. Finding a workable parental balance for the kids will require adult behaviour from you both, which means you need to be civil with each other. Ultimately, if there is no civil agreement between you the court will eventually find one which will be in the best interests of your kids. The longer the war rages, the more limited the court outcome will be. The more considered your proposed parenting plan is, the better your chances of becoming more than just a weekend dad.

The changes made to the Family Law Act in 2006 were progressive, to say the least, but they don't come with guarantees or a set of steak knives. What the amendments do is create the opportunity for shared care arrangements and equal parenting time, normally over a week or a fortnight, if — and it is the mother of all ifs — there is a real likelihood that the orders will be maintained. The court, in all cases, would prefer that parents come to their own arrangements, and sometimes the fear of the court's consequence is enough to turn the most stubborn parent around.

"The best-case scenario is ultimately the one that can be agreed on. Failing that, it's what the court can construct from the arguments presented to it."

The best-case scenario is ultimately the one that can be agreed on. Failing that, it's what the court can construct from the arguments presented to it. To ensure the outcome is as equitable and practical as possible you need to get all the necessities in place. Getting Jane, or the court, to seriously consider what you offer as a solution is vital to the success of your case. The more toothless your tiger is, the more affection it may receive, from those who remain argumentative or are influential in determining how much of a best-case scenario this turns out to be.

39 The afterlife in the Land of Jane

Golden rule 1: 'You both think you're right.'
Golden rule 2: 'Show me you have the time.'
Golden rule 3: 'Show me you have the place.'

Was it all just a bad dream? I'm afraid not. Welcome to the afterlife, the new, yes new, relationship you have with Jane. Don't sit back and think this is going to be a holiday with all meals and accommodation provided. That might have been the previous relationship you had. Don't panic, it's not a boot camp and there's no sign that reads 'Welcome to Hell'. You're in a place of limbo, somewhere between a bad dream and the never, never again. Where's Jane, you ask? Oh, she'll be there when she wants to, or if it suits her. You may not know where things stand with Jane or where they are headed, but don't rush, tread lightly and just remember to put one foot in front of the other.

The afterlife with Jane is what you make of it. The less time you spend venting the disappointments of your former life, the sooner you'll move on. You can't change a rocky past, but you can smooth out the future. What Jane does with the other 99 per cent of her life is not your business, and really the same goes for her. There is, however, one mitigating factor — your children. The situation she finds herself in is not your concern or responsibility. Yet your kids certainly are, whether it's written down in a parenting plan or not. You're still their dad, or at least it should say so on their birth certificate.

The afterlife you now lead with Jane doesn't need to pick up where you left off, with obscenities flying back and forth. Really this new relationship needs to be simple, and for blokes this can be a blessing in disguise. The longer relationships last, the more complex they become. It's not just all the water under the bridge or down the drain; it's the wear and tear that may have you feeling a little ragged. Blokes don't like their relationships looking like a bird's nest of fishing line. We'd much prefer them to be tight and straight. So as the starting flag drops, and the afterlife begins, stop thinking about bringing any old habits to this one.

"From day dot in the afterlife in the land of Jane, documenting communication is important, even when you're barely on speaking terms."

From day dot in the afterlife in the land of Jane, documenting communication is important, even when you're barely on speaking terms. If arguments are entered into, then enter them into the book of the afterlife only. This record may support any claims you make in the future, so it's something worth doing now, and forever after. Time, place and a description of the conversation is all an entry needs to be. It's a record more than a story, so you don't need to yell action, cut or roll the tape, as much as you need to document what's been said and done. The most important topic that should appear in this book of the afterlife is what you discussed with Jane concerning your kids. If it begins to read like a Mills and Boon novel, then the accuracy and effectiveness of this document may be diluted.

> "Keep it simple in the afterlife with Jane, and keep it about the kids."

Keep it simple in the afterlife with Jane, and keep it about the kids. Work at it to make it work, for everyone's sake. Don't argue with her. Commit the fights to your past, though you don't really have any say whether Jane will or not. Be agreeable, firm, calm and committed. Don't get all hemotional about it, or be seen to be taking. All you want to do is share what you need to share with her and keep it about the kids. Be the one who says little, but records in detail. Be calm, but most of all try to maintain the peace no matter how thin the air becomes. If you do lose your cool in the afterlife, you may lose your opportunity to communicate and possibly precious time with your children.

40 Going around again

Golden rule 2: 'Show me you have the time.'
Golden rule 3: 'Show me you have the place.'

Getting back on the horse and building a new relationship can be a double-edged sword these days, but don't let this deter you from searching for some happiness. Re-engaging with the dating scene may or may not be an issue for you, but if a long-term thing is what you're after, you may be a little more cautious going around again. If girls just want to have fun, then enjoy their company; just don't be too quick in deciding this one might be the Ms. Right. It is vital that you remain buoyant throughout this ordeal, and a bit of fun is good for you. But it may be best to keep it casual — at least till your parenting issues are sorted.

"Some say kids complicate things, and they may, but they don't mean to."

Some say kids complicate things, and they may, but they don't mean to. How much you consider your children in how you go about the business of establishing new relationships is important. Keeping things simple initially is the key. Rushing an introduction to your kids is always a risk. Firstly, they might not be ready to embrace someone new, as you have. Secondly, you may not be able to predict their reaction. During such a complicated period of your life, and arguably a very fragile time for your kids, it's best for all in the long run that you keep things simple and separate. If you feel an introduction to a new flame is the right thing to do by your children, then make sure she is a long-distance runner and not just along for the ride.

If another woman was a big reason for your separation, then an introduction is probably not a good idea. It's inevitably going to get back to Jane and could cause a reaction. If you have decided to reinvest, that's your decision, but how this impacts on your kids will be portrayed by Jane in her affidavits. So to minimise this chapter in her paperwork, really consider whether introducing another woman into this equation is going to complicate things and possibly hurt or at least confuse your children.

So if you are game enough to go swimming in the deep end again, it may be best to keep the kids out of it, at least until you have resolved things with Jane. If you are adamant that your new flame is future partner material, and they wish to assist in providing care for your children, then this may be a good thing, especially if your kids are accepting types. Just be aware of the wrath of Jane. Any of the good work you have done to mend bridges may be washed away and down the drain. Apart from the fallout that rains down on you, your kids will definitely not benefit from any further complications or instability. Going around again may seem like a good idea but there's a time and place for everything.

41 Cultural considerations

Golden rule 1: 'You both think you're right.'

Australia is a cultural crock pot simmering away, all day, every day. Our country is a landscape built on beliefs and customs from just about every race that walks the Earth. Places of worship are plentiful and diverse, catering for just about every religion practised these days. There's also a fair chance these days that the cultural heritage of Jane is different from yours. There may be only one majority, but several minorities make this nation a whole. In Australia, there is a very real possibility that the culture and beliefs you have and practise will differ from your parents', and this may also be true for your kids.

"Whether you consider this to be good or bad depends on how judgemental you want to be."

Whether you consider this to be good or bad depends on how judgemental you want to be. In this situation, you are better off leaving the judging up to the ones who do it for a living. The one thing you may have overlooked in all that's going on is the culture of your children. As a parent, whether you're in a position of caring for them or not, it may pay great dividends to spend some time considering what beliefs you would like your children to hold, and which, if any, religion you would like them to practise. Faith is a personal thing, but religion, in a sense, is universal. What child should go without the opportunity to experience, practise and understand their cultural heritages? It's not a matter of ostracising them from the other side of their family, but they should have an opportunity to know and practise your faith. This can often be overlooked during all the mud-slinging, but it is something worth spending some time on and considering.

From fundamentalists to atheists, these days this country caters for just about all. As a parent, you may be able to offer your kids knowledge of cultural practices that Jane cannot. Of course, this may also be true on her side of the fence. Articulating to the court the cultural and religious beliefs you would like your children to practise is something the court may consider and encourage. Creating the opportunity for a child to learn of their heritage is something the court may believe is important. This will not be set in stone, but culturally disadvantaging a child is not something a court is designed to do. So it is worth tabling your wishes, whether or not your beliefs are held by the majority. If they offer your children some guidance and direction in life, they will probably be considered, perhaps more than you might believe.

42 Saving a few shekels

Golden rule 1: 'You both think you're right.'
Golden rule 2: 'Show me you have the time.'
Golden rule 3: 'Show me you have the place.'

Your struggles will cost you in ways you cannot imagine or budget for. The extent to which this experience will diminish areas of your life, and cripple you in others, will depend on how and where you choose to invest in this campaign. The true cost of it all may never be fully quantified. Sure, there are the bills that can be totalled, and the time you missed with your kids can be calculated, but the damage it does to you personally and socially is difficult to evaluate.

The situation will come to feel hopeless if you let it. It could cost you tens of thousands of dollars, and destroy longstanding relationships, if you allow it to. Ultimately, you have the power to decide how much this is going to cost, but you may not yet have that insight. The best way to limit the carnage and cost is not to fight. Don't let your hemotions run the show, and don't give up. Be an active agent of change, someone who is willing to make a contribution, not just a donation. Digging your heels in, or sitting back and hoping for an armchair ride, won't get you far. You can pay through the nose for representation if you like, but it is the contributions and concessions you are willing to make that will produce results. Be proactive. Take the lead. Ask for advice and be aware of any consequences before making decisions. It's going to cost more only if you choose to throw the first stone, or something that's hard to retract in the future, especially if it crashes through the front window of the family house.

Being proactive and pragmatic will save you money, which you may be able to spend on more constructive endeavours, such as your children's education. There is a fine line between being proactive and obsessive, or over the top, during these hemotionally vulnerable times. It's critical to inform your legal counsel honestly, even if you aren't particular proud of your actions. Your counsel is there to represent you, not to judge you. If you fail to disclose information that may not shed a great light on you, Jane may do it for you. You might think this is saving a few shekels, but having to explain yourself later will inevitably cost you more time and money. Pointing out the errors of your ways is just as important as blowing your own trumpet of parenting virtues. Honesty is always going to be the cheapest option.

It's the facts that matter, not your emotions. It's not easy to separate the two, and that's ultimately why you need representation. Putting things off or into the too-hard basket isn't going to save you a dime. The quicker you come to the realisation that having a slinging match on the footpath with Jane isn't helping your cause, the better off everyone will be. Many blokes believe in reason, but there are so many hemotions that weigh down the facts and prevent a solution floating to the surface. Any cost associated with your case should be related to achieving some form of resolution or agreement. Any currency you spend outside this simple logic is a waste of time and money and may create further costs.

Be prepared, and prepare as much information as you can for your solicitor. Don't be concerned about detailing your feelings; everyone knows you're hurting. Spend the time (and money) on facts, dates, times and actions. A record of events is far more valuable to your case than a truckload of how this makes you feel. Your counsel may ask you *why* Jane won't allow you access to your children, but *how* events have led to this situation is more important to your case than the pain and suffering it has caused.

Be a realist. The one who stands up straight and is always willing to work to find a solution will come out of this much happier in the long run. You are not together anymore, so you need to act and think independently, but you don't need to be her polar opposite. The truth is, you and Jane may be on the same page on some things, and light years apart on others. The more you resolve the ball-park issues, the more runs on the board you will have. Just don't waste time and money arguing about semantics and petty points of conjecture. Agree on what you can, but don't argue about what you can't. Simply agree to disagree and let the solicitors work those things out.

> "The longer this saga runs, the more it's going to cost you."

The longer this saga runs, the more it's going to cost you. That's a fact, not an outcome. The longer you let the situation fester, the more it will cost to resolve. The more you let your hemotions run the show and call the shots, the bigger the bill is going to be. So before you get on the phone and let your solicitor know how long it's been since you've seen the kids, think about whether or not you're just wasting time and money. While there's so much disagreeing and arguing going on, the chance of an eleventh-hour miracle or change of heart from Jane will remain minuscule. Unless there is some new development that your counsel needs to be informed about, don't go jumping on the phone and ringing them as if they were a help line. Your actions may meet your hemotional needs, but you need to trust your solicitor's strategy and adhere to their advice.

A counsellor is far better equipped to help you with hemotional issues. If the whole thing is seriously doing your head in, don't be shy to put your hand up for advice. Sometimes seeking help to manage your hemotions successfully will save you more than just a few shekels. Men's groups may also provide some sanctuary for little or no outlay.

This situation is not likely to right itself, and neither is a single person, no matter how much you pay them, going to make it all go away. That's your job, and the more you do your job rather than your block, the more money you will save. You can prevent this process breaking you and your bank balance. It depends on how pragmatic and cooperative you choose to be. Because the more you agree to with Jane, the more time, money, health and happiness you'll end up saving.

43 Grizzly bearing the cost of it all

Golden rule 1: 'You both think you're right.'
Golden rule 2: 'Show me you have the time.'
Golden rule 3: 'Show me you have the place.'

There's no price you can put on your children, but you can guarantee that although they come free of charge, they will cost you time and time again. That said, they provide you with plenty of gold to go along with the grief, and being there in the front row of your child's life is a truly rewarding experience. Expressions like 'money well spent' don't sit right when it comes to grizzly bearing the cost of it all. Perhaps 'whatever the cost' is more applicable to this situation. It's certainly not a game for gamblers. But those who are willing to invest some effort and trade in massive amounts of patience may end up with a fair return.

"You might pay for quality work, but really what you are doing is funding someone else to do the agreeing."

Your expenses depend directly on the amount of arguing you wish to do. The more you fight, the more you pay. The less you tolerate, the more you pay. The more you disagree, the more you pay. It doesn't matter which way you look at it, the sign reads the same. Argue at your own cost. How much do you really want to wager on an argument with no favourites or guarantees? Whether or not the gamble pays off, the cost of it is hard to count, let alone make sense of it all. The taxing effects on your health, mentally and physically, of maintaining a rage or argument can also be costly. Fighting's not great for the appetite or diet either. It will leave you tense and cause a real headache or even a heart attack. If you had the foresight to see what the true cost of this would be, you might not end up grizzly bearing the cost of it all.

Even the richest are fiscally challenged by this process. The numbers do add up . . . and up and up and up. What you may originally have been quoted has a good chance of blowing out, depending on how many detours are added to the journey. Realistically, if you have something tucked away for that rainy day and you are determined to fight, the forecast is likely to include a down pour. A healthy investment is one that returns fortitude to your character. But the greatest investments are made with the best of intentions and good will. Whatever the scale of your expenditure, there's no guarantee of a return. You might pay for quality work, but really what you are doing is funding someone else to do the agreeing.

Ongoing compulsory support payments for your children are determined based on the amount of care you give and your income. As a parent you want to care for your children, but your source of income must also be protected at all costs. Maintaining a career or job is vital to service the costs of your case and to guarantee your ability to afford a good home for your kids. Allowing the tension and stresses associated with your situation to impact on your work and health is like carrying an injury into a football game — it's only going to get worse. By the end of the game you'll probably find yourself hobbling about on the sideline, with only a spectator's role to play.

> "Money is not a bargaining tool, and children aren't for rent."

It's not a good idea to let Jane know how the costs may be crippling you, or how much economic discomfort this is causing. Money is not a bargaining tool, and children aren't for rent. If Jane is withholding the kids, she won't want to lend anyway, no matter how much of a gravy train you think she's on. Both user and non-user pay in this business of arguing over children. The income earners may be the ones who end up bearing the cost of it all. But your children can't afford for this to be happening. It is always cheaper in this situation to agree rather than disagree. There's far more happiness in a resolution than there is in war. Regardless of the result and their own wealth, many fathers can still be heard for many years grizzly bearing the cost of it all.

44 Going the distance

Golden rule 1: 'You both think you're right.'
Golden rule 2: 'Show me you have the time.'
Golden rule 3: 'Show me you have the place.'

It's difficult to say how long a journey like this will take or how much it's going to cost, tax, frustrate, possibly humiliate or age you. Every bloke's story is different, and so are their endings. One thing they have in common is eventually they all reach an agreement of one kind or another. Whether the end result is best for their kids and what they wanted is probably debated over many barbecues in back yards across this wide brown land. But if you are to reach any kind of agreement, a fair amount of compromise will be required.

It's your kids you are doing this for, and that should remain the theme of your campaign. If you remain focused and keep bringing the conversation back to the kids, your discipline will serve you well. It doesn't matter if Jane wants to take a swipe at you or is not answering your phone today. There may not be much of a view to enjoy, but pushing Jane over the edge is only going create delays while they dispatch a recovery team to find her. Just about everything you do along the way will need to focus on the interests of your children. Showing Jane and the courts that you can provide a safe and secure environment and are willing to put significant time into your children will certainly help along the way.

"Just about everything you do along the way will need to focus on the interests of your children."

Ultimately, it will take as long as it does to resolve your parenting issue. If you cannot achieve this in a civil manner with Jane, or through formal mediation, then the courts will look for a solution that will minimise future conflict. It does take a while for your day in court to come and your matter to be heard. You need to pace and brace yourself along the way. There will be times that seem to take forever and then there will be moments that simply fly by. But whatever trials and tribulations you face, make sure you stay focused on what's best for your kids.

It may take your all to travel this course, and will require you to make significant investments and commitments for your children's future. But do what's necessary to clear the fog so the sunshine can return to your day. The limit to the cost of it all will be determined either by your bank or by your ability to reach an agreement with Jane. Rather than maxing out your credit cards, ask your solicitor to estimate a ball-park figure, and if need be go and get a loan. You can spend a small fortune just getting to court, and as long as fires burn the bills will rise. Just remember, every time you fight with Jane it costs you time and money. Every time you agree, you save yourself heartache and possibly a big debt.

"But patience is a steadfast companion and the more you lean on it, the smoother the journey will be."

However long it takes to reach an agreement, make sure you're prepared to go the distance. Patience is the best friend you can have along for the ride. There will be many times when your hemotions will have had enough, and you'll think the world has gone mad. But patience is a steadfast companion and the more you lean on it, the smoother the journey will be. It's hard to be a tourist and observer of your own life especially when this situation will undoubtedly reshape it. Listening and considering what is said along the way is far better than reacting or fighting time and time again. Even if you spot the fat lady in the distance, be patient and allow the process to come to an end. Going the distance isn't about coming first or winning the race. It's about arriving at an agreement in the best shape possible.

THE LAY OF THE LAND

45 Paying for it

Golden rule 1: 'You both think you're right.

We live in a world where the user pays, whether we like it or not. Gone are the days when you had change from a big day out. If the absence of your children isn't just and grates on your masculine sense of logic, then prepare to have it aggravated even further by what they call Child Support. Here in Australia our government has developed a system of child endowment that can be the result of little more than Jane's bad behaviour. You only have to think about it for a second to hear the footsteps of dread running up your spine. Chances are, once separated from your children you are or will be socked for their maintenance without having a say in how it's spent. It's a bit like paying tax, and any bloke who's worked a day in his life has done that. The ATO don't send you a bill for a new road or a hospital — they simply calculate what you owe them. This comparison doesn't relate to the rate charged but the fact that you have to pay it without knowing how or where your dollars are being spent. You're told you are providing for your kids, but in reality no one can guarantee your hard-earned money is spent on the welfare of your children.

"It would be good if you could allocate your funds against services for your kids, like swimming lessons, extra books, braces, school fees or music lessons, by just ticking a box like ordering a hotel breakfast."

It would be good if you could allocate your funds against services for your kids, like swimming lessons, extra books, braces, school fees or music lessons, by just ticking a box like ordering a hotel breakfast. Things don't seem real fair in parenting, and they aren't. Nothing's 50/50 when you count the costs and not just the dollars and sense of it. This is why it's so important to rein in the amount of emotional energy you choose to expend. Be patient and save it for your kids and a time when you are able to unlock that door in your life again.

Nothing is ever 100 per cent; even the smartest kids at school sometimes got it wrong. Like everything in life, unless you make the best of it you may not enjoy it. There is a way to spend your hard-earned dollars and gain a foothold in the decision making for your children, but this path you and most fathers seek is more like a jungle trail than a highway. As with many times on this journey, you'll have to tread a straight and narrow path. If you stumble you'll need to pick yourself up, dust yourself off and get back on track again. Whether you think it's right or not, make sure you pay Child Support. It may not be just, but it's a sure sign to the court that, regardless of current circumstances and how you have been treated, you remain a giving parent and able to provide for your children.

If you are self-employed you should sit down with your number cruncher and work out how this payment may affect your business and impact on your cost of living. The tighter you can pull in the belt, the less painful the debt will be. It's so important to bed this one down and not let the debt mount up. Don't be suckered by Jane into just giving her the cash. Make it formal, even if it remains a private arrangement, and let Child Support know. One trap not to fall into is the couple of months of back pay she can claim. The trick here is to get it sorted first with your accountant, second with Jane if you can, and finally with Child Support.

If you are able to leverage any kind of agreement with her it may be through the financial support you provide for your kids. It may sound crass, but money talks. Even if you can come to a private arrangement, Child Support will undoubtedly make you and Jane aware of how much they think you should be shelling out. There's no escaping the cost of kids, but what you see as a negative to your bank account is actually a valuable investment for the future. Having a private arrangement means Child Support won't be hounding you if a payment is missed, which can at times get quite impersonal and insensitive.

"Pay it, and it will pay off for you in the long run. Don't pay, based on some stubborn principle, and you will create a world of pain for yourself."

Pay it, and it will pay off for you in the long run. Don't pay, based on some stubborn principle, and you will create a world of pain for yourself. Though you may not be able to stop Jane buying herself something from your payments, know this: quality of life comes at a cost, and supporting children is what a parent is supposed to do. The best outcome for your children is for their father to be adult enough to accept an arrangement that will create opportunities for them and demonstrate to the court that, regardless of what's happened, you remain a reliable provider.

46 Stuck in the middle

Golden rule 1: 'You both think you're right.'
Golden rule 2: 'Show me you have the time.'
Golden rule 3: 'Show me you have the place.'

Although legal aid is a mechanism to support people who can't afford a solicitor, it may be of little use to you. If you work full time, forget it. If you have assets, forget it. If you are not receiving welfare, forget it. It's a real life catch-22. If you have no income, you may be fortunate enough to receive legal aid, but how on earth is a judge then going to believe that you can adequately support yourself and provide for your children? Jane may claim to have survived on little to nothing over the years, and yes, love is free, but everything else costs money. If you do have an income, even if it's not a six-figure salary and even with the potential expense of this exercise, legal aid won't be footing your bill. The courts may absorb some of the costs of the process, but not your personal legal expenses. It seems to cost nothing to have little chance and a lot to have a good chance, and those stuck in the middle end up paying for the best chance they can afford.

If you are afforded this little legal luxury (most argue it's a right), the common assumption that you will get an inexperienced solicitor is generally incorrect. You may be surprised at who does legal aid work. In some instances, it may even cover the costs of a barrister to present your case. Sadly, most single fathers, if dutifully employed, will find themselves exceeding the threshold for legal aid support. It is a little worrying and hardly just, however, if legal aid affords Jane representation that is well beyond your budget. Still, legal aid is an avenue worth exploring, even if you think you're probably ineligible.

> "To make sure the costs of being stuck in the middle don't blow out, join the fast lane and start agreeing."

What's more likely is you're lined up with most fathers who are stuck in the middle. You may be solely financially responsible for funding this challenge, but even if Jane has qualified for legal aid, she won't be afforded any luxuries. There is a way to get a faster result and reduce the expense, though. To make sure the costs of being stuck in the middle don't blow out, join the fast lane and start agreeing. Checking out of this situation will occur when an agreement has been reached. The express lane out of the middle of this costly legal mess, which no one can really afford, is by way of a simple agreement. If being stuck between a rock and a hard place is not where you want to be, make a conscious decision to put the cheque book down. Because the longer you fight, the more this will cost and the longer you'll remain stuck in the middle.

47 The boys in blue

Golden rule 1: 'You both think you're right.'
Golden rule 2: 'Show me you have the time.'
Golden rule 3: 'Show me you have the place.'

Avoid them as you do, the boys in blue can also play a part in what can be an intricate web of games. If these gentlemen and women introduce themselves into your situation, then it's a pretty good indication that things have gone pear-shaped. If the police do come a knocking, don't answer the door with your ego. This is no time to stage a scene from *Braveheart*. Rather, a calm and collected approach to the visit will serve you best. The hardest part to stomach in this scenario is that they will state they are just doing their job. Even if it's obvious to all that they have been made a pawn in a parenting battle that has been waged for many months, possibly even years, always behave in a civil manner.

The police are not your enemy, so don't go second-guessing why they are there. Let them in and let them explain; seeing the home environment might answer their questions faster and see them on their way. Parents have been known to abuse child safety services, making complaints to trigger a visit. Child safety officers are a special breed and, like police, should be handled with extreme care. Just try your best to avoid an argument if their claims are misplaced, far-fetched or even absurd.

"If the police do come a knocking, don't answer the door with your ego."

Don't honour ridiculous claims or try to launch a campaign of your own. The boys in blue will investigate only one matter at a time. Be pleasant, show concern but don't be arrogant. Again, you need to stay calm and use the situation to your advantage. A good report back to child safety may see them scrutinise the next complaint more closely. If you get a visit once, don't be surprised to see them again. If you established a good rapport on their first visit, next time you may not need to guess where the complaint has come from.

Police and government department officers are not rocket scientists, and they often continue to entertain charades for longer than they should. This is not a game of logic, or one you want to play, but as long as you put out the spot fires that break out along the way, there will be no harm done. In managing your behaviour and the insults, you will gain strength, skills and friends. Remember that police are people too. They are also fathers and mothers and do have some experience in matters like these. Unless something has gone seriously wrong, they haven't turned up to take your kids, so don't panic. You won't need to put them on your Christmas card list, but the faster they see your cooperative side, the sooner they will be on their way.

48 Who asked you, child safety?

Golden rule 1: 'You both think you're right.'
Golden rule 2: 'Show me you have the time.'
Golden rule 3: 'Show me you have the place.'

Any man with a sense of pride will hardly be thrilled by the prospect of having to spend time entertaining these impersonal people. Never in your life will you be paired with such a bizarre dance partner. It is hard to fathom how a government department can swoop down on you like a hungry eagle after a new lamb and begin levelling all kinds of accusations at you. But these people do. Whether or not you are known among your mates as a bit of a twinkle-toes, if asked for a dance you better know your moves and not just the moon walk. Let them lead, and if you are blessed with two left feet and are known for putting the odd one in your mouth, perhaps seek some counsel before stepping on their toes.

"Their focus is on the children's welfare and wellbeing."

As a parent, you would be well within your rights to ask how a government department holds the interests of your child higher than you. Or how often a government department is going to tuck your kids into bed, read to them, kick the ball with them or help them with their homework. But sadly, it isn't about these things. Their focus is on the children's welfare and wellbeing. If Child Safety have contacted you, then it's likely somebody has complained that you and/or your environment is a risk to your children. Now that you have reopened the book after hurling it against the wall, you need to see this small hurdle in the context of the match. It's time to bring your competitive edge to the fore and understand the game. Ironically, what kills spiders is fly spray. The secret to doing this dance with these welfare officers is to allow them into your parlour to snoop around, listen carefully to their questions, answer what is realistic, and choose not to respond to fictitious claims and statements. The situation you may find yourself in is no laughing matter and can seriously damage your parenting aspirations. So keep your head up, back straight and look them in the eye.

It may be best to give the house the once-over before they arrive. Make sure you have the jug on. Let them try all their tricks, like the good cop, bad cop routine. It's often nothing more than a Bonny and Clyde cross-examination kind of production, but the worst bit is you'll have a front-row seat. You may need to seek support to dodge some of their bullets. But rearing up like a brown snake is only going to fuel their fire and fill their reports with unpleasantries about you.

Be the fly that has ingested the poison and let them feed on you and leave them to deal with the person in the mirror. Rather than bearing the emotional brunt of their questions, use the opportunity to read between their lines of inquiry. The more you interpret rather than respond to the questioning, the more benefit there may be for you. Don't be afraid to ask your own questions; just don't forget to answer theirs. The more cooperative you are, the faster the experience will be over. Be prepared, as always, and don't come empty-handed to an interview either. Make it known to them if you believe your case for the care of your children seems to coincide with their inquiries, because it won't be the first time they have been put in this position. Ask them what options you might have to make your own complaints, but don't fall into the trap of playing tit for tat.

This government department is doing the right thing by investigating a claim of child abuse. It may be Jane who is doing the wrong thing. It's important not to confuse the two actions as being one in the same. If someone has raised questions about your children's safety, then don't be so naive as to think that the system is not being misused. Don't be defensive, be forthright and paint a true picture of your family life. Explain the simple things, like routines and day-to-day activities, and you'll probably answer more of their questions than you realise.

> "Don't be defensive, be forthright and paint a true picture of your family life."

If they come to visit with back-up in tow, don't be defensive or circle the wagons around the kids. Your name's not Custer and don't make it your last stand. Procedure is procedure to them, so instead of panicking, simply observe the way they approach things and the tone of voice they use. A bit of respect may earn you some level of admiration in return, or at least soften their tone. They may never be your friends, but you don't want them as enemies. Their powers are extensive and can be wielded instantly. Just be cool and remember, an elephant never forgets. If you play this one well, it may come back to bite the hand that was feeding them. Dancing with the devil will get your fingers burned, but trying to go toe to toe could see you end up in hell, and that's no place for anyone to be.

49 Caution, DV court ahead

Golden rule 1: 'You both think you're right.'

The Domestic or Family Violence Court is a bit like a women's fashion boutique with the power to convict. It's no place for a man, though many have had the experience. It's a busy place, which doesn't say much about how we act towards one another. Welcome to Behaviour 101 for Dummies. The idea that your hemotional actions can be seen as criminal is a frightening consequence of this fashion bizarre. If there was a level of dispute that was abusive, aggressive or threatening in parting ways with Jane, then it's more than likely you'll visit this little shop of horrors.

If you think giving Jane an earful and sending text messages or tweets are not violent things to do, guess again. Violence is not just the physical harm of another. Just about anything that was said as a threat or hurled in anger will be listened to by this court of unfortunate circumstance. Apart from an additional case and expense you may not have seen coming, this is a place that's to be avoided like the plague. Children blame the one who started it; this court holds adults accountable for their actions and hands down criminal convictions. If you have been on the receiving end of a battering, proof from a hospital or a police report is important. For in this court there is plenty of *he say, she say, hearsay.*

"If you think giving Jane an earful and sending text messages or tweets are not violent things to do, guess again."

Having a history of being hunters doesn't help men; neither does the fact we are known for going to war and have a reputation for being the more aggressive sex. They say the stats don't lie, and if you try to here there's a good chance you'll become one. Do your best to avoid this place, where the cards and odds are heavily stacked against you. If you are on your way, some female support other than your solicitor is a good idea. But remember, court is no house of fashion. Comb your hair, have a shave, remove the jewelry, buy a pastel-coloured shirt, put on some brown leather shoes and get your mum to knit you a vest. If you have a pair of coke-bottle black rim glasses, whip out the contacts and reattach your magnifiers, because your appearance before the judge needs to be as inoffensive as possible to at least soften the blow.

Don't go betting the judge will understand your side of the story, not when over 80 per cent of men who have experienced domestic violence in Australia have never bothered to tell theirs in the past. We guys just don't have the numbers. Though the DV court can't make a ruling giving you access to your children, be aware that if Jane is claiming you are a threat to your children, DV orders can be made to include your kids.

Bad behaviour is not good, but it happens, especially when separation occurs in a family. If you think anything that goes on in the home stays in the house, you're wrong. Though police can be reluctant to engage in civil disputes, there are most certainly criminal consequences that can result from a short visit to this house of pain. So if you are to make an appearance, make sure you look as inoffensive as you can and don't forget some female company. This is a ring you definitely don't want to enter. It's certainly no place to carry on fighting, so be prepared to agree to some sort of formal civil order. There's a time and a place when you need to stand up and be a man, but the DV court is one place you don't want to have to do it.

"Bad behaviour is not good, but it happens, especially when separation occurs in a family."

50 You say, she say, hearsay

Golden rule 1: 'You both think you're right.'

It takes two to tango, and to have an argument. One normally instigates it and the other usually retaliates. Like watching a game of tennis, it gets pretty boring seeing people do the same thing, over and over again. Judges have probably heard more arguments in their time than they care to remember. So, it's nothing new or surprising to them to hear yet another bitter dispute between two parents over access to their children. What's done is done, but what you do now will hopefully be more successful than your relationship with Jane. As long as argument exists in what's left of the relationship, there will be little chance of resolution. The tit-for-tat tennis match of *you say, she say, hearsay* is about as entertaining to the court as watching the grass grow.

Hopefully, you have laid your case, good bad or indifferent, on the table for your counsel to see. And Jane has probably done the same on the other side of town. Embellishing on events is unwise, as what could be construed as a simple lie may be considered a crime in court. It's called perjury, and it's something you definitely don't want to do. Depending on the nature of your disputes with Jane, the court may decide a number of things. In many instances, Jane's and your name calling may simply cancel each other out, especially if it sounds like a lot of hot air. But if it presents as abusive, then it's more than likely the court will want to know more. The truth is, the more you sling it, the more it's going to cost first to hear and then to resolve.

The nature of the ruckus recorded in your affidavits will of course be of great interest to the court. If you and Jane can't agree, then the court will be the one to determine what is best for your children. It will view your battles with Jane seriously and will aim to protect your kids from physical and psychological harm, including being subjected to or exposed to violence, abused or neglected. So the more you choose to engage in arguments that are often no more than hearsay, the more you are likely to damage your case and your chances of parenting your children in the future.

"If you and Jane can't agree, then the court will be the one to determine what is best for your children."

Arguing may be a dance you've performed with Jane in the past, but if it looks like continuing to cause damage, especially to your kids, then regardless of who said what, the court will ensure that the opportunity for future parental disputes is as limited as possible.

51 What's up, Doc?

Golden rule 1: 'You both think you're right.'

One thing you can be assured of is how thorough the court will be in leaving no stone unturned. So if you think hiding something is doable, guess again. Whether you are asked to take drug tests or see a mediator, psychologist or psychiatrist, just do it. Cooperating with the court is always a good thing to do. No matter what you may think, what the judge thinks is best is best. This is not to say what you think is best for your kids isn't as important; more to the point, this is what a judge is there to consider. But what is asked of you, no matter how much it may feel like an insult, needs to be done, and with a smile. A judge will always want to be more than certain and often their requests will put to rest arguments or accusations made against you.

If you are sent for some kind of test or interview, or mediation for that matter, don't be late or look untidy or hung-over from the night before. If you are a little nervous, try to keep your hemotions under control. The more cooperatively you approach what could be a humiliating experience, the better it will be. There's no need to personally justify why you're there. These matters are always conducted on a need-to-know basis, and are handled in a professional and clinical manner. There is nothing to fear, though it may be the first time you have had the pleasure of a drug test or interview with a psychiatrist. Just be diligent and agreeable in your responses. As confronting as drug tests or seeing a shrink may seem, both are non-confrontational experiences, so there's no point creating one by riding in on some high horse.

"Keep It Simple Stupid."

If the intellectual challenge at hand is causing you some anxiety, take a deep breath and use the KISS formula: Keep It Simple Stupid. Answering questions can be as simple or as complicated as you want to make it. But the more you say, the more that will be recorded, which may lead to further questioning. Being honest won't hurt either; after all, the truth is a simple thing. It might stir a few emotions, but do your best to keep it together. If you're inclined to shed a few tears now and then, tissues will be made available, or you can bring your own. Whatever the court asks you to do, again just do it and smile. Really, it's a small hurdle in this steeplechase and just another obstacle your ego will need to overcome during this ordeal. The more dignity you have, the less humiliation you should feel, and if you are feeling that way inclined, here's hoping it's remorse rather than guilt.

The best outcome you can achieve in these types of situations is the satisfaction of extinguishing allegations made against you. Silencing the critics is one thing, but carrying out the requests of the court is the most important thing. Failing to do so will have consequences and will only lead to further speculation. So put on a smile, but don't grit your teeth, because what doesn't hurt you will only make your case stronger.

52 A quantity of quality

Golden rule 1: 'You both think you're right.'

Choosing a solicitor to represent you is a bit like buying a car. Not that many legal eagles would be pleased with this comparison. Solicitors, whether new or used, come in all shapes and sizes and with a range of optional extras. There are makes, models and styles to suit all tastes, so there's bound to be one for you. When it comes to cost, not many of these vehicles have a capped price or service plan, though you can sleep easy knowing whatever you purchase should be dependable and reliable. How much you end up spending is your choice, but it's money well spent if it goes the distance.

Finding a solicitor is like visiting a car yard. Yes, there are a lot to choose from but you'll need to test drive them first. Taking a few for a spin around the block to find the one that handles the conditions best, even if you are sobbing on their desk, is so important. What you're looking for is a measurable amount of emotional investment, not just a letter of the law and here's your bill means of transport. You need to look under the bonnet and see that there is genuine interest and belief in what you're saying. Chances are you may get a bit emotional during consultation and a bit of compassion by them may galvanise your working relationship. It's up to you to choose a ride, but you need it to be dependable and reliable in any situation.

> "Finding a solicitor is like visiting a car yard. Yes, there are a lot to choose from but you'll need to test drive them first."

It's not just trust or money you put into a solicitor like fuel. You want to be paying the ferryman, someone who will go the distance, advise you, take instruction from you and keep motoring. Most first appointments with solicitors are free or discounted, so it can pay to shop around, if you're prepared to part with a few shekels. It's impossible to test drive every model out there. Instead, use the goldilocks theory: all you need to do is find the one that feels just right. If your ride is too big or too small, too hard or too soft, you'll need to find a different make or model. Often the flashy new ones aren't worth their price tag; maybe the one that's been round the block a couple of times is more what you're really looking for. They say you can't pay for experience, and court time is a very valuable and important feature. Newer models may be faster off the lights, but all cars need to obey the speed limit. There's no point ending this race in a smoldering heap by the side of the road with the finishing line nowhere in sight.

Your solicitor may put a clever argument to the court, but an argumentative approach is a sign that this lawyer doesn't have many miles on the clock. The best models are the ones that have all the features you will ever need, including the ability to navigate pitfalls, take an insult on the windscreen, gently reverse when need be and deliver you on time every time without the feeling of being thrown around the back seat like a rag doll. A cooperative vehicle is going to be far more economical and effective in what can be a hostile and costly environment. You're not looking for grunt or turbo-charged performance so much as a smooth ride.

"You're not looking for grunt or turbo-charged performance so much as a smooth ride."

If you seek luxury, then you'll end up with a very expensive ride. There are certainly no lemons at the top of the legal tree, but turning up to court in a limousine is a bad look, especially if Jane arrives in a rented legal aid hatchback. It also pays to ask those who have driven down this road before what make and model they used for this journey. How their ride performed can certainly offer a valuable insight before you go making any kind of investment. There are so many vehicles available, you are bound to find one that will take on your case. Just don't be fooled by guarantees, because there are none. What you need to do is feel comfortable with your purchase, knowing your ride has some miles under its belt, has delivered others safely to their destinations, is easy on the fuel, makes little to no noise and is low on emissions, especially in a tight situation. At the end of this journey you want a car that will go the distance. Whether you do it in style or on a budget is neither here nor there. What's important is that it handles all conditions, no matter how slippery or rough the road gets, and that you arrive at an agreed destination in one piece.

53 Which way, boss?

Golden rule 1: 'You both think you're right.'

There aren't many who will like this comparison either, but your solicitor is a bit like a taxi driver. At the end of the day they can only take you where you want to go. Like a good solicitor, a taxi driver knows what's happening on the streets, understands the rules of the road, gets you there as quickly as possible and hopefully delivers you in one piece. Whether or not you know which way to go, your solicitor will always have their own view on proceedings, but they may be less likely to voice their personal opinion than a cabbie.

There is a certain duty of care your solicitor needs to abide by. They are charged with the responsibility of acting on your behalf at all times, representing your interests to the best of their professional ability. This is another clear distinction between a cabbie and a solicitor. Though they are driving things for you, and their knowledge of the road ahead is far superior, you still remain in control of the wheel. But, apart from fighting with Jane, overruling your solicitor could well be the stupidest thing you can do. When it comes to the deal that needs to be struck, your solicitor will hopefully be turning on the charm and doing their utmost to reach an agreement. You do need to understand where things are going, and you can't afford to sit back and enjoy the ride, but barking out directions like a back-seat driver is not a good idea.

If you do agree to take a certain path, stick to it, because changing direction is not only a bad look, it may prove difficult to amend and only add further costs to your trip. In short, be aware and confident before agreeing to anything. Although the finish line may appear to be in sight, you need to make sure you are working with as opposed to dictating terms to your solicitor or simply riding on their coat-tails. It's a difficult dance to do, especially with something that's so personal. But giving an instruction should be a considered act, not an emotional performance. It's not so much a matter of knowing when to hold 'em or fold 'em as it is a matter for discussion and dialogue. Firstly, it involves listening to what your solicitor's saying. Secondly, you need to understand what's being said. Thirdly, you need to make considered decisions and lastly give clear instructions.

"lastly give clear instructions."

By the time you get to the negotiating table, hopefully you'll have developed a reasonable understanding and working relationship with your legal counsel. It is really important to remain on the same page as much as you can. If you're not a rocket scientist, don't forget you are paying them. So ask questions, because you need to understand what's going on. There may come times when all you get from your solicitor is an inquisitive stare while they wait for you to provide them with instructions on how to proceed. But always remember, whether or not you know which way to go, like a taxi driver they will hopefully get you to where you want to be.

54 Counting the cost of it

Golden rule 1: 'You both think you're right.'

Obtaining care of your children is an expensive exercise, often misguided by hemotions, which makes this a doubly costly process. There are a number of things you can do to keep a lid on the outpouring of funds. The first rule to maintain a positive balance sheet is to minimise the costs of arguments, which are like throwing money down the drain. If you choose to fuel a fight, then enjoy the merry-go-round as your costs will spiral. It's not that solicitors overcharge you, but they will bill you for every minute and word of their service. The truth is, an argument is only going to delay an outcome and the sooner you reach a solution, the sooner the legal fees will end. Love may be free, but kids come at a cost.

> "Money will always be better spent on your kids rather than on an argument with Jane."

Even when you have reached agreement, court costs could also become a personal expense. Money will always be better spent on your kids rather than on an argument with Jane. It's also more rewarding to be shelling out for them than funding a war of words, numbers, dates and times with their mum. Nobody really knows why solicitors and barristers are so expensive. Some say it's because they are the ones that clean up other people's mess. Others say it's because of all the time they have spent on learning the law. There's a more than a bit of truth in both points, and other reasons for sure. In hindsight, what you are paying for is the experience that's required to gain a fair result. So the more proactive rather than reactive you are in resolving issues, the better value you'll get for your dollar.

You do pay for quality in this world, though your case does not necessarily have to be a huge expense. Dollar for dollar, you want to be paying for experience in these matters. That's where you'll get the bang for your buck. An experienced lawyer knows what rules apply and how to reach an agreement. There's a simple equation with two known factors for calculating costs: kids cost money + arguments cost money = costs a lot of your money.

Your legal representative, unless provided by legal aid, is going to cost you. But hopefully they will be able to do what you have not, and that is create an agreement and resolve you're parenting issues. If you think solicitors are weapons of mass destruction you're mistaken, so using them to wage war is pointless. Though they will argue your case, in reality they aren't there to argue with anyone. Resolution is the art of the great legal mind and hopefully that's what they will achieve. There's simply no point funding an argument, especially when there's kids involved.

55 It's nothing personal

Golden rule 1: 'You both think you're right.'

What could be more personal than the future of your relationship with your kids? The answer is probably going to be nothing, but allowing your hemotions to be involved during this process is not a good idea. Written in the pages of Jane's application to the court will be information that you may consider private. But once in the hands of her legal team it will probably be aired and may be personally very hurtful. You will need more than a grain of salt to help digest what is said about you in court, but reacting to what is said, is of no help at all.

"It is no surprise to the court that you and Jane can't or won't agree; they deal with this every day of the week."

At this time it's best to act like a duck and allow the water to run right off your back. Jane's solicitors, like yours, are just doing their job and as hard as this is to stomach, you must swallow your pride. Jane is going to have a different take on things from yours, probably on everything, but just stick to your story, because that's what you will be instructed to do. Just remember, the court realises that both parties think they are right, but so often the conflicting arguments, and often that's all they really are, cancel each other out. Court is not a game of he say, she say and it's not there to take sides. Believe it or not, the court is trying to find a solution, to have both parties to agree and come to an arrangement that's best for the kids.

It is no surprise to the court that you and Jane can't or won't agree; they deal with this every day of the week. But the court is a place of resolution, so the sooner you pick up on this vibe the more effective the court will be and the sooner you'll get a result. Your situation is like a car that is bogged and the court is a tow truck. It may pull you out of the quagmire, but once you're mobile again the court expects you to move on under your own steam.

Recognising that Jane has some good qualities does you no harm. Informing the court of her good points, and hopefully she has some, will show the court that you are not as one-eyed as a pirate. Even a newspaper, though often full of doom and gloom, still has a good story among its pages. Despite the pain and suffering Jane may have caused or inflicted, it is worth mentioning to your solicitor some of the qualities that attracted you to her in the first place. While you're at it, you may as well list some of the finer points of your own character that Jane was attracted to. This isn't a beauty contest; it's not about appearances so much as personalities. The clearer picture of Jane you can paint for your solicitor, the more insights they will have and the more they will have to work with. Nobody likes to be left in the dark, so keeping something from your solicitor, whatever it might be, is of no benefit to your case.

"Sticks and stones are not permitted in the court, so let Jane's words reflect her character and let yours do the same for you."

Despite what may be said about you or how you are portrayed by Jane, smile, because it's only their opinion. How you present is far more important for you. Be comprehensive and be prepared to disclose the good, the bad and the ugly, but don't get too personal or take it to heart. Keep things above the belt and never lower your guard. Show no hemotion over what is said about you. When your character is being questioned be silent and solid as a rock. Sticks and stones are not permitted in the court, so let Jane's words reflect her character and let yours do the same for you. The judge has an educated mind and has literally heard it all before. Let your solicitor do the talking, because that's what you're paying them for. Just ensure that your story includes the good times as well as the bad, and swallow your pride, even if it is hard to digest.

56 M&M&M: Method and the madness of mediation

Golden rule 1: 'You both think you're right.'

Before you have your case heard in front of a judge in the Family or Federal Magistrates (Circuit) Court, you will need to go to mediation. Although you may consider it madness, mediation is the likely and preferred method of resolution of your parenting dispute. If you fail at first to reach an agreement, don't be surprised when the court recommends mediation once more. If Jane is the argumentative and uncooperative type, mediation may seem like a great big waste of time, but it's not. This game is about patience and, in the end, coming to an agreement. Always take a positive attitude into discussions and maintain this disposition, for it will serve you well.

It is far more beneficial to be agreeable than to use this opportunity to vent your frustration or anger. Mediation is a chance to sort things out and to reach agreement on care arrangements for your kids. The more you remain focused on this idea, the more likely you are to find a solution and reach an agreement. It's the unknown that drives a bloke to drink, so mediation should always be valued, and it's also far more expedient and cheaper than a court case.

"Mediation isn't a test or an inquisition; it's a civil way to have your parental views considered, and most importantly, to reach an agreement with Jane, even if she's not in the same room."

Mediation isn't a test or an inquisition; it's a civil way to have your parental views considered, and most importantly, to reach an agreement with Jane, even if she's not in the same room. Mediators are not referees, and they're not there to judge you. Their role is to help both parties come to an agreement, which is often no picnic. Mediators aren't there to take sides or gang up on you with Jane; they aren't the ones who have created the problem. But they can help resolve it, so be nice to them at all times.

There are two things you need to do in mediation. First, you need to know what you think is best for your kids. This may sound simple, but your hemotions can be quite distracting during negotiations of the heart. Have a clearly defined position on what you're prepared and not prepared to concede ground on during discussions. If you think what you want is what you will get, think again.

Concessions are a given in any negotiations, including mediation, so be cooperative but don't compromise yourself or what you honestly believe is best for your kids.

Second, always remain positive. If the mediation session looks like going pear-shaped, don't spit the dummy. Simply smile and remain positive. Knowing how far you're willing to bend will help you hold your ground. Even if that sinking feeling begins to take over, try your very best to remain polite to all parties, especially the mediator. It's okay not to agree, but all good negotiations end in some form of consensus, which may simply be that you and Jane are unable to reach an arrangement this time.

Mediation isn't over in an hour or a day. It may consist of several meetings and conversations, so it's critical to your success that you remain positive, leaving the door to resolution open. Eventually, if a care arrangement is not agreed upon, the mediator will be required to submit a report to the court for consideration, and the judge will certainly pay attention to their opinion. So be nice or risk someone other than Jane painting a grim picture of you.

If you're being represented at mediation, allow your solicitor to do the talking but pay attention to everything that's said. It's important always to agree with them before agreeing with anyone else in the room. Their experience and skills are what you're paying for, so allow them to do what they do best, no matter which way you think the mediation session is heading. Mediation is a really good opportunity to table what you believe is best for your kids, whether or not Jane likes what you say. It is also a fundamental and integral part of Australia's family lore of the jungle, these days. Most of all, remember it's always better to be able to walk away with your ego a little bruised but your dignity intact, than to storm out, your hemotions ablaze and smoke bellowing from your ears.

"Concessions are a given in any negotiations, including mediation, so be cooperative but don't compromise yourself or what you honestly believe is best for your kids."

57 McContact centres

Golden rule 2: 'Show me you have the time.'
Golden rule 3: 'Show me you have the place.'

The last place on earth you would wish to visit is jail, but coming in a close second are places known as family contact centres. These necessary evils are the only spaces in which some fathers get to see and communicate with their children. These cold, sterile, unnatural environments are the destination of parents who behave badly and are unable to reach agreeable parenting solutions. Rather than pandering to Jane's bad behaviour, if these places are all that is offered, then in the interim you may be better opting out.

If faced with the prospect of parenting from one of these places, you might be jolted into thinking that there has to be a better option for your kids. But, depending on your past or recent behaviour, this might be all that is afforded. If so, you might be better off trying to work on the communication front with Jane to achieve something a bit more hospitable for your children. Finding another solution is not about turning down an opportunity to see your kids; it's about whether you're prepared to subject your kids to that kind of environment. Children are like sponges; they will soon pick up on the vibe and probably ask why there is a security guard standing in the corner?

The other major problem with these facilities is they are normally booked out months in advance. So before you go agreeing to use one of these centres you should inquire about the waiting list and when an appointment might be available. If you choose not to subject your kids to this rather surreal experience, then maybe Jane will rethink her less than reasonable solution. Having standards and exercising them is something you should be doing, adhering to and falling back on throughout this ordeal. It's not about raising the bar but about a way for you to show a mediator or the court what you stand for and want for your children. Unless you are found to pose a real threat to your kids, it would be reasonable to assume that somewhere in this wide brown land would be a place other than a contact centre where you could enjoy your children's company.

If Jane is resisting giving you access to your children, then maybe somewhere public, like the local park or McDonald's, would be suitable for the kids. Yes, that's right, the mighty golden arches. Who would ever have thought that a fast-food restaurant could become the largest unofficial centre for contact and handovers for families in Australia? But when you think about it, Maccas is better equipped, and more enjoyable for kids, than any family contact centre. All suburban McDonald's have restrooms, playgrounds, indoor and outdoor tables and chairs, food and drink and a security guard, plus there are always local police passing through taking advantage of their discount cards. There's also ample parking available. If you can maintain a civil disposition and are prepared to engage in some constructive parental dialogue, you may find the attractions of a McDonald's family restaurant will melt Jane's icy disposition. Surely a clown with red hair, red nose and big red feet could provide a warmer, more suitable parenting environment than a government institution?

58 The courts: a real family affair

Golden rule 1: 'You both think you're right.'
Golden rule 2: 'Show me you have the time.'
Golden rule 3: 'Show me you have the place.'

It may come as a surprise to you, but when you were trawling for a solicitor you might have noticed just how many legal eagles practise family law. That's because 18,000 new disputes over the care of children are heard in Australian courts per year. Knowing this, it is not surprising that so many partnerships and marriages these days end on a sour note — in separation or divorce. You can at least take some heart from knowing you are definitely not alone.

If the courts are where your case is destined to be resolved, it is worth making a trip into town to see just how busy these places can be. You'll be lucky to get a seat, but it will give you some idea of what goes on, so when it's your turn it won't seem so alien. The flurry of solicitors and, to a lesser extent, barristers outside court may also provide some insight into how many cases seem to be resolved at the eleventh hour. It's not a magic trick, but rather a recognition of the consequences of relying on a court case that can assist you and Jane to come to some agreement instead. This is always the preferred option rather than needing a judge to clean up the mess that's been created.

Life in the courts is so busy these days that parenting problems are heard by both the Family Court and the Federal Magistrates (Circuit) Court of Australia. The more complicated the matter, the more likely it will be heard in the Family Court, so make sure your solicitor knows which one is right for you. Matters involving more than one child and family assets are generally heard by the Family Court. The more complicated matters are, the longer they will take to resolve. The Federal Magistrates (Circuit) Court is much the more expedient path and hence may be a fair bit cheaper in the end. Either way, it's a very expensive process, so the more you can resolve without the court's assistance, the more change you'll have at the end.

"The more complicated matters are, the longer they will take to resolve."

Don't think for a moment that Federal Magistrates are any less experienced or competent to deal with your case. It's because of the sheer volume of cases these days that the Federal Magistrates (Circuit) Court also deals with parenting matters. Regardless of which court you appear in, the process, if it needs to go to the judge's decision, will take more than one hearing to resolve. Due to the number of cases and the length of time they take to resolve, parenting orders may be made on an interim basis as the case proceeds.

> "The courts these days are a family affair, though they are not really a place for children."

Given the flow of traffic through these places, it definitely pays to be on time or, better still, early. You'll most likely spend much of the day waiting in the comfortable lounges in the court foyer for your 15 minutes of fame, but hopefully your solicitor will be using this time to try to strike a deal with Jane's counsel.

The courts these days are a family affair, though they are not really a place for children. It's handy to bring along someone for support and to keep the nerves under control. A family member is handy, but bringing the new girlfriend may not be the best idea. It is also ill-advised to try to make small-talk or engage in conversation with Jane. It is far better to let your solicitor do the talking at all times. Avoiding confrontation at court is a must. Often you can cut the air with a knife, and it may take no more than a throwaway remark to spark a bushfire in the foyer. If you can't behave yourself in the judge's house, then what will the court think of your claims to being a responsible parent? Just stay calm and in control, whatever you do, to avoid becoming more of a conversation topic than you already are.

ANIMAL BEHAVIOUR

59 Speaking of Jane

Golden rule 1: 'You both think you're right.'

How you speak of and with Jane, and the language you choose to use, can be either your undoing or mightier than any sword you hope to wield. Obviously, some words have been said in the past. Before you go telling her how it is, tell yourself there is a better way. As with many aspects of this process, the sooner you get your story straight, the better it sounds. Separation causes uncertainty and unnecessary anxiety. It can cause your hemotions to spill over into ridiculously misguided actions, which are of no benefit to anyone. By speaking hemotionally, all you convey (and not very well) is your pain and hurt. Choosing to think before you speak with Jane will produce far better results than simply flying off the handle.

> "Language is made up of words, and the ones you choose should be valued and never wasted."

The way forward might be straight to anger management classes, but there is a smoother path that's more like a walk in the park than peak hour traffic. Choose to be polite and pick your words carefully. Keep conversations focused on the kids, not Jane's likeness to a dairy cow. The rule of thumb to follow in all conversations with Jane in the afterlife is to try to speak to her with the same kindness and gentleness you afford your children. This may not be easy but it's a sure way to see how being polite can make a difference. If you apply this to the job at hand as you work to get your kids back, you'll reduce the chances of further arguments, uncertainty and disappointments.

The tone of your voice should be pleasant to hear. Like an Irish ballad, your delivery needs to be on time every time, and the love you have for your kids should be evident in every line. Remembering to think about what you need to say, before you speak, is critical to the success of every future conversation you have with Jane. The same is true when you're speaking of her. Don't let your darkest thoughts become a description of your children's mother. If you are generally struggling to find something nice to say about her, you are better off saying nothing at all.

Language is made up of words, and the ones you choose should be valued and never wasted. It's better to believe things are improving than to speak of your pain or the hardships Jane has heaped on you. It's not even worth saving the misery for mates' talk; you'll just end up ridiculed for being soft. Your patience needs to be endless, and your tolerance for insult high. Don't lose your cool and allow your language to end up in the gutter. Commenting on Jane's less attractive attributes should be kept to a minimum or preferably kept right out of the conversation. There is no point calling to remind her of faults, mistakes and shortcomings. Hopefully these less attractive attributes no longer cloud your day. You're calling to speak to the kids, to find out how they are going or to arrange some time to see them. Every time you speak with or about her, you can choose to build a way back to your kids or build her case against you.

"Kindness may not get you everywhere with Jane, but it may get you some time with your kids."

It's not about sweet talking her round; just be polite and keep it civil. Lose the limited opportunity to communicate with the gatekeeper to your kids and the damage you sustain can be considerable. Kindness may not get you everywhere with Jane, but it may get you some time with your kids. Showing her one card of respect rather than your whole hand is so much easier and more productive. Think before you speak and keep it polite with Jane today, so there'll be another opportunity tomorrow.

60 What's best for the kids?

Golden rule 1: 'You both think you're right.'

Who's to say what's best for your kids? Nature intended that there be two decision-makers. But when it comes to the courts, ultimately there may be only one. If the two creators cannot agree on what's best for their kids, then inevitably someone must ultimately decide. It's like a spaghetti western stand-off with a conspiracy theory, except while cowboy and cowgirl face off in the street, both end up shot by someone on a grassy knoll. Although there was a need for only two in the bed, in the event a pillow fight erupts, a third party may end up deciding what's best for your kids, whether you agree or disagree.

Three is a crowd and if you're off to court to have your case resolved, you can bet that although it's a very private matter there will be a number of people along for the ride. Suddenly something so personal as the welfare of your children is going live. Is this what's best for your kids? Sadly, it may well be. If Mum and Dad aren't talking or are still fighting, then at least your children still have another option. Whether you carry most of the blame for the separation is not the issue. Getting a plan that produces parental continuity is what's best for the kids.

What's best for the kids is more than a question; it's an indication of where answers to this epic challenge lie. It's also your best response to Jane during any disagreement. Stick it on the fridge to help you stay on course. If both of you can agree on this simple priority, then there is a real chance you can agree on others. If what's best for the kids is all you discuss with Jane, then there's less chance she'll be dragging up the past or hurling abuse at you. If you stay on this yellow brick road, it will help all involved, and your kids can find a way home.

If you're the only one willing to walk the straight and narrow, don't be concerned, just lead and others will eventually follow. As a parent, if you continue to show, time and time again, that your focus is on the welfare of your children, then it will become evident to the court. It's about setting a tone and taking a stance in this match before a ball's bowled. There may be only one side playing cricket, but despite the body blows continue to stand your ground. Let history show your actions were just and that you were prepared to do what was best for your kids.

"If you're the only one willing to walk the straight and narrow, don't be concerned, just lead and others will eventually follow."

It doesn't matter how many times you ask this question, the answer is never equal to one. This may at first be hard to digest, but what's best for your kid's is, consensus between their parents. It may be left up to the kids to decide but, although their views are valid and should certainly be considered, making children choose, put simply, is passing the parenting buck. After all, parents are supposed to parent. They should know and always do what's best for their kids. Keeping the afterlife with Jane about the most important common denominator is of benefit to all involved. As parents, you and Jane have a responsibility to care for your children, and with that comes the right to decide what's best for them. But if you and Jane won't or can't agree, then the courts may end up deciding for you, or rather for your kids.

"As parents, you and Jane have a responsibility to care for your children, and with that comes the right to decide what's best for them."

61 Sharing is caring

Golden rule 1: 'You both think you're right.'

Sharing is caring, and caring these days is all about sharing. Shared care arrangements are recognition of equality in contemporary parenting, though what is equitable may not be based on your parental desires, but rather on what is equitable for your children.

This is where the odd bloke has ended up in a world of hurt — understanding that equitable does not necessarily mean equal. You need to accept this, to understand the logic of it. If you're in denial, read on. Men and women come from different planets, or so it's been said. We are different, and often worlds apart on some issues, though it is often said that some guys listen like women. How two different things can be equal is more ideal than logical. Things are not and may never be equal, and neither is it a good idea to measure your parental importance against Jane's. Parenting is not an exact science or a competition, it's about personal devotion.

But all is not lost, because equality can still be your friend. To develop equality in the parenting of your children, you may have to bleed for it. But you will be part of the decisions that shape your kids' future. Brokering ideas with Jane should always be in the best interests of your children. What you think your kids might like to do, where they might go to school, what they should and should not eat: sharing these concerns is the simplest way to avoid parental confrontation. It's not what you want, it's what you think the kids want or need that counts. Just as you have separated from your wife, separate yourself from your hemotions and keep the conversation focused on the kids.

"Just as you have separated from your wife, separate yourself from your hemotions and keep the conversation focused on the kids."

If you and Jane can't be together, it's more than likely your kids will enjoy time with their parents separately. It is hard enough for an adult to get their head around this idea, let alone a child who will have to learn to live with it. What's really at the heart of sharing the parenting of your children is cooperation. For without it there is little likelihood a shared care arrangement will ever be agreed on. The more you consider the idea of equality for your kids, the more you will realise that it's not as simple as a 50/50 split or a one week on, one week off kind of arrangement. Sharing is caring and the more you are able to do this with Jane, the better off your kids will be.

62 Oh me, oh my, oh our

Golden rule 1: 'You both think you're right.'

Communication is the key ingredient in the cake of goodwill that you need to begin baking. Without conversation you will either be paying for your solicitor to write letters or left in the dark. As costly as they can become, your solicitor is there to try to establish a rapport with Jane's representative, to begin peace talks and work towards a resolution. One tip to reducing the damage to your finances if you can't converse with her directly is to write to Jane. But before you run for the ink and quill, you should think hard about the language you intend to use. Even if you feel you're on the outside, and you may well be, try to be as inclusive as you can. (You may also want someone to check your spelling before popping it in the post.)

Communicating with Jane can take a number of forms, though smoke signals aren't that good for the environment. There are more contemporary methods of ensuring she gets the message. But whether it's a phone call, email, text, voicemail or tweet, you run the risk of wielding a double-edged sword. The upside of a message as opposed to a conversation is that you can convey what needs to be said to Jane without raising your voice. You can announce your arrival at handovers without having to knock on the door, and if you receive a poor response you will have a record. Even if it's not what you want to read, keep them — don't delete them. The downside to these digital communications is that Jane will also have a record of what you say. So to avoid the damaging and embarrassing, think before you tweet, and re-read your messages before sending them. Another flaw with these new technologies is you have no excuse for not picking up the phone or getting the message.

> "The upside of a message as opposed to a conversation is that you can convey what needs to be said to Jane without raising your voice."

To make these types of communications work, you need to keep them charged. Don't play the battery was flat card. Ignorance is not bliss when it comes to keeping the lines of communication open. Worse, Jane may start doing the same. The secret to getting to see the kids is keeping as many lines of communication open as possible, and if this means establishing them, then do so. Buying a mobile for Jane and the kids is a real investment into building a safe and secure way to speak with your kids, or at least to know their whereabouts. A tip is to get a capped plan, so you can limit the financial damage and ensure the line is always open. Also, get it insured in case a conversation heads south and the phone is thrown out the window, along with your hopes. The key to good communication is taking the time to choose your words. Be it spoken, written or any other form, the language you develop for Jane can determine how often you see your kids. Using some possessive language is not recommended under any circumstances. The old *your* and *my* scenario only creates the opportunity for a difference of opinion when what you're looking for is a consensus. Be inclusive in the way you communicate with Jane and keep it about the kids. Don't let your hemotions do the talking. Keep the conversation civil, polite and to the point. Do most of the listening, and don't forget that expressing gratitude and the odd thank you can go a long way.

The key word in your child-oriented conversations with Jane is *our*. She didn't conceive them on her own. This three-letter word has real power if used well, and at the very least it will remind her that the kids were not the product of immaculate conception. Our kids, our children, our bundle of joy are all inclusive terms that put you back in the picture. There are many more seeds you need to plant, but not as many as the beans it will cost if you lose the ability to communicate with her. Reminding Jane that it was from you that the seed of life originated, not her girlfriends or her mother, relates you to the kids and reminds her that she is not alone in the parenting department.

> "The key word in your child-oriented conversations with Jane is *our*."

Referring to the children as 'our' in your affidavits is also good practice. If you do end up before a judge, it shows that you're not the one in denial. Using possessive 'I' and 'my' arguments is charged with hemotion. So practise it till your gums bleed and 'our' will serve you well. It is the key word in all conversations you and Jane will have about your children. It is an inclusive agent that articulates to the court your maturity and may just unlock Jane's sense of humanity. But be warned, anything you say, and the way you say it, write it, text it or tweet it, that is abusive may be used against you. If you need any motivation, just imagine your children are eavesdropping on your conversations with Jane. Think before you communicate, be inclusive rather than exclusive, plural rather than singular, and choose your words very, very carefully.

63 Did someone ask for make-up?

Golden rule 1: 'You both think you're right.'
Golden rule 2: 'Show me you have the time.'

They say there's something positive you can gleam from any situation in life. It's not so much about being an optimist as it is about developing pragmatic awareness. Only you really know how volatile things have become with Jane and how easily she's baited or will explode in a certain situation. Most importantly, you are really the only one who knows where she is likely or unlikely to concede ground in the parental turf war. Fortune-tellers aren't much help; not even they can predict how long this battle will be waged. This simply depends on how long it will take you and Jane to reach an agreement or for the court to hand down a decision.

"They say there's something positive you can gleam from any situation in life."

Small gains often go unnoticed by those who don't pay attention to detail. If you choose to be diligent and note down your disappointments, then you may find the total sum in your parental account has some currency with the court. If you record each time you asked and were denied time with your children, then at the very least your efforts will be noted by your counsel and the court. A log of rejection will:

a. Show you have tried to make time for your kids
b. Document when you were denied time with your kids
c. Record Jane's unwillingness to support your parenting proposition.

The process of logging and documenting requires a steady hand and the ability to resist biting the hand that can feed your parental hunger. Live to fight, or rather not to fight, another day. Instead, choose to log it in the hope that this record itself will help reunite you with your kids. If you can maintain your composure by focusing on the job at hand, then you will have something to show for your effort other than your disappointment. Patience is required. If you don't know what this is, take up fishing. It's an art that needs time and is not easily acquired, so you may as well make the lesson as enjoyable as possible. The syndrome of being let down time and time again on this journey can, if managed with little hemotion, prove to be a rod for Jane's back. It is always best to keep your requests reasonable, civil and within business hours. One o'clock in the morning is not a good time to be texting or phoning repeatedly. You've probably more chance of waking up the kids, and apart from it being a nightmare to get them back to sleep, Jane may return the favour by creating a few sleepless nights for you. If you go throwing stones into the water you'll only create ripples and disturb the fish.

If, by chance, Jane involves the boys in blue, at least you'll have a record other than your phone data. By keeping your inquiries civil, they are more likely to be seen as reasonable.

Even if Jane does like to hang up, think twice before ringing her back. A DV or AV order is not going to help, may create a very real parental barrier in the Family or Federal Magistrates (Circuit) Court, and will undoubtedly make your parenting situation more complicated and harder to resolve. Pushing Jane and the envelope will only end up costing you more time and money in court to resolve your parenting matter. You don't want to let her off the hook or allow her to score cheap points.

"Pushing Jane and the envelope will only end up costing you more time and money in court to resolve your parenting matter."

With some small wins under her belt and the wind in her sails, have no doubt, Jane will develop an unassailable confidence. This is the one thing you must try to avoid at all costs. It's simply too costly and ultimately something you can't afford. The feeling of emptiness that can kick in when she pulls the pin on a visit, or takes off with the kids on holidays or at Christmas, may be unavoidable. If it does occur, then at the very least it needs to be noted and submitted for a mediator or a judge to see.

Make a record of Jane's actions and behaviour, but make sure her records on you don't include police reports, DV orders or convictions. If you keep the hemotions under control and show you were denied access to your children unreasonably, then the court may decide that make-up time is in order to re-establish relationships with your kids.

Hemotionally, dealing with separation from your kids can be very difficult, but physically it's very simple to be pragmatic and patient. Just remember to:

a. Write it down
b. Keep your cool
c. Be persistent, not a pest.

You know Jane best, what makes her tick and what makes her bite. But in this parental struggle you'll need to show others, be it a mediator or a judge, that you're a person of patience and not easily baited.

64 C'mon already, and a little thing called graduated care

Golden rule 2: 'Show me you have the time.'
Golden rule 3: 'Show me you have the place.'

If, through no fault of your own or even because of something you did, your children have been under Jane's lock and key for some time, don't worry, it's not going to help. One of the worst hemotions of all is the fear of uncertainty; it can make a man waste a lot of energy and think up some pretty stupid ideas. Whether Jane has come to her senses, or has agreed during mediation or has been ordered by a judge to give you access to your children, there is a rule of thumb called graduated care that might come into play.

This little ideology works on the theory that when reuniting a child with their parent, a gradual approach to re-establishing and rebuilding the relationship is what's best for the child. Though it hardly seems ideal, and may rub against the grain of your parental logic, it's what experts say is best. It's also what the courts practice, so if you can see it as a way forward, it's a very good opportunity to demonstrate your parenting prowess. This entire process is an incredible challenge for all modern Australian fathers. However, the rewards for demonstrating patience are enormous, and failing to do so can be devastating.

"Although the war may not yet be over, making gradual care work is a wonderful way of showing Jane, a mediator or a judge the benefits of their decisions."

If it is ordered by the court that a gradual care arrangement be put in place, you can claim a small victory, but don't let anyone witness your song and dance. There are a few traps involved in this kind of arrangement, and some real benefits too. Importantly, it will specify when and where you'll be seeing your kids. You should be able to schedule your time with your kids, which will give you the opportunity to think ahead and plan some activities. It will allow you to regain some continuity, knowing your time with them will be regular and will increase in the future. Although the war may not yet be over, making gradual care work is a wonderful way of showing Jane, a mediator or a judge the benefits of their decisions. What's also important is to document these times.

This is handy to show Jane if she has doubts about whether your daughter can ride a horse and to start filling picture frames around your new home.

> "The last thing you need to do is fuel Jane's fire by pointing out the damage she has done to your relationships with your children."

There are a few traps, however, like calling for equal time from the outset. This isn't what's being offered or how things will play out. Allow time to be built up and don't let your kids down. The last thing you need to do is fuel Jane's fire by pointing out the damage she has done to your relationships with your children. If you fail to agree or meet these graduated obligations, then it's possible less care will be awarded to you in future. It's not a good idea to try to reschedule dates and times either. Stick to what has been agreed, do a good job of it and make it work for all involved. Fail to do your part in the arrangements and you run the risk of looking like a father who puts his kids second, which is not a good look for you or a place they may want to be. Try your best to be patient and allow time to gradually heal your relationships, because time is now on your side.

65 Dressed for success

Golden rule 2: 'Show me you have the time.'

They say first impressions last, and they're right. Although court is no house of fashion or opportunity to parade around, some real consideration should be given to the image you present in court. You may receive instruction on appropriate attire for your big day, but just in case, make sure your outfit does not stand out in a crowd. Fashion statements are best left for catwalks and the streets. Whether it's good or not, your taste is not going to win you any points, or a score out of ten from these types of judges.

Instead, here are a few simple tips. Wearing the colour red is not recommended; the colour of war is simply not a good choice. Unless you're a matador who's due to perform immediately after the hearing, it is strongly advised that you go for something a little less confrontational. Keep the graffiti on the streets and not stencilled all over your outfit. The promotion of labels and fashion logos should be kept to a minimum or out of court altogether. Expressing your identity through the fashion style of a subculture will not help your case either. Clearly, the message here is leave the material girl in the closet. It's not about looking like you just stepped out of a fashion catalogue, and nor do you want to look like someone who just crawled out from under a rock. It's not about your ability to accessorise or the latest man fragrance, though you don't want to turn up smelling like a sewer either.

> "Keep the graffiti on the streets and not stencilled all over your outfit."

Dress as though you're going to the most important job interview of your life, minus the tie. Simple patterns, like softening checks, are preferable. A good-collared light blue shirt and a jumper may give you that clear-sky look. Dark blue, grey or brown trousers are good options and often look smart. Avoid black and no, no, no jeans, no matter how expensive, cool or comfortable they are. Leave the sneakers at home by the back door, and wearing boots that make you look like a biker are also ill-advised. Be a chameleon, not a peacock. Blend in, look serene, quiet, peaceful and a little soft around the edges. Let your quiet side do the talking, after all judges' robes don't look to have changed in the last century. Take the time to consider what you wear on your big day, because first impressions do last and you want to be the kind, reliable and considerate parent, not the coolest bloke in town.

66 Deal or no deal

Golden rule 1: 'You both think you're right.'

Without a doubt, the most important order you can issue from the battlefield is the ceasefire. This doesn't mean you should drop your guard, but when a deal looks to be on the cards, it's time to pay attention to what's being said and written. Tell your hemotions and man-feelings there's nothing to see; you don't need a back-seat driver or distractions from the audience at this time. Don't bother calling for the throne either, and get down off your high horse because righteous is not what you need to be. This window is not going to stay open for any great length of time. Using it to grandstand may see the opposition withdraw an offer, batten down the hatches and prepare for war.

Apart from all the work your solicitor has done to compile the best case for the care of your kids, the opportunity presenting itself should not be wasted. Hopefully, you have the requirements of golden rules 2 and 3 in place and have developed a clear proposition for Jane on how a parenting agreement may look and work. The worst thing you can do is diverge from this, or send your solicitor on a kamikaze mission with potentially explosive demands. Although you may have been on the outside, this is neither the time nor the place to presume that because your parental rights have been acknowledged you can act like a bull in a china shop. Quite the opposite, you actually need to tread very softly. The door may appear to be open, but really it's only ajar. It's best to allow your solicitor to work the negotiation rather than barging in on the conversation.

Never see eleventh-hour parenting negotiations as a waste of time, even if you're minutes away from finally having your case heard by the court. Like boxing, it's best to end the fight as opposed to letting it go to a judge's decision. If what is being offered is more poultry than roast chicken, and your solicitor agrees it is not even close to a reasonable proposition, then there's little you can do but bow politely and enter the court. It is so important to stand your ground and not accept a less than equitable solution, because you, your kids and Jane are going to have to live with it from that moment on. No matter how much you want to see your kids, don't let your hemotions trick you into accepting an agreement that won't sit right with you or might cause regret in years to come.

"Like boxing, it's best to end the fight as opposed to letting it go to a judge's decision."

Although you may be feeling like a basket case, drained and depleted by this ordeal, leaning on your solicitor at this time is the best thing you can do. That's why you have them there in the first place. The best solicitors are highly skilled in negotiating a solution, and at this time you are best going to your money (wo)man to make the play that may end this game. Being part of your children's future is the long-term goal. How you get there may require a number of clauses, concessions, compromises and a certain amount of graduated care. As long as the end goal is the same as, or close to, what you proposed for the kids, be prepared to concede some ground to finally reach an agreement.

"To accept an agreement outside of court is a far better outcome than having the court do it for you."

Don't rush things if the end is in sight — be the old bull and walk down the mountain. To accept an agreement outside of court is a far better outcome than having the court do it for you. If you are to act like a parent, then the responsibility lies with you to do what's best for your kids. The same goes for Jane. But how she acts and what she's prepared to concede and accept is outside of your control. Really, all you can do is know what you want and be determined to achieve this even if it includes months of graduated care and means you are the one doing all the driving. Ultimately, you will have to wear it, so the more you can shape it, the more comfortable a fit it will be in your life.

THE END OF THE TALE

67 The big day

Golden rule 1: 'You both think you're right.'

Sooner but what can seem much later your day in court will come, and with it your chance to be heard. If today is the big day you probably slept little last night. Out of the million and one possibilities, scenarios or outcomes you may have come up with in your head, there is likely to be only one and that will belong to the judge. If you have your house in order, your big day may bring about some changes. Every father's situation is different, for one reason or another, though all who have their day share the same issue: they both think they're right. Appearing before the court isn't a measure of success or failure. After all, if you both didn't think you were right, you wouldn't be there at all. Then again, the courts already know this and therefore are willing to provide some unbiased assistance to resolve this for your kids.

> "Many a good man has fallen by the wayside, so it is an accomplishment to have made it this far."

Many a good man has fallen by the wayside, so it is an accomplishment to have made it this far. In doing so, you have brought a factor to your equation who has the power to answer your questions and change your parenting situation. If Jane has reigned over and dominated the parenting scene, and your house is in order, there's a good chance her days of flying solo are up and some orders, even if temporary, will be made. One way or another, your solicitor and Jane's could be instructed to broker a deal. It may not be everything you want, but it could be a chance to reunite with your children. To have brought your situation before the court is at least a small victory, if you need to see it that way. But the judge isn't there to hand out awards for effort. You may both be convinced you're right, and you're in the right place to be heard, but the truth is you're both wrong to argue. You're also wrong to think court is a place to fight. It's not so much game on as game over. The only winner should be the kids. All that's needed for this to happen is for you and Jane to start being cooperative.

Like a good boy scout, be prepared to be shunted to another day to be heard. Perhaps the court has other matters that must take priority, so the judge may decide not to lift the lid on your can of worms today. Don't take it personally. Take a look around and you'll notice it's standing room only on any given day. All's not lost if your case is set down for another day. Today may have been a shock to Jane's system, and might be enough to bring her to her senses. Judges are experienced in these matters, so be patient and see how things play out. Whether you agree or disagree, realise it at the time or not, in the judge's house, they are the only ones who are right.

Hopefully you will blend in, look inoffensive and smell good on the big day. There's no need to be consuming espressos or cans of Red Bull while you wait. It's not a good look to appear edgy or be seen bouncing off the foyer walls before your case is called. If you like your music, don't be adding 'Eye of the Tiger' to your playlist either. It won't be helpful. Though your solicitor (or possibly barrister) is paid to work on the day, it's no armchair ride for you. You're employing them to do a job and they will require your attention and input throughout the course of the day. Smokers, wear a patch, because you can't be ducking out intermittently to escape the place. You need to be still as a rock and remain present at all times.

With a bit of luck you remembered to turn off the hemotions and ego along with your mobile when you entered the building. Be attentive at all times to what your solicitor's saying, even if you don't like the news. It's not a good look to let anyone see you wincing at a proposal. If your solicitor is open to discussions, they may end up doing more running around than a water boy. Don't become demanding or negative during these negotiations. Simply agree to allow the discussions to develop. To get some sort of deal as a temporary order is a start, and testament to your counsel's cooperative nature. There's give and take in all negotiations, and if it does not completely extinguish what you consider is an equitable arrangement, at least entertain it. The most important thing to remember is to listen to your solicitor. You are paying them for their advice and representation.

The moment you walk into the court, you need to be cool, calm and collected. Allow your solicitor to instruct you where to sit, and from the moment your arse touches the seat say nothing unless asked. Looking around and having a sticky-beak or waving to a supporter in the back row is not a good idea. You're in the judge's house now. Sit up, shoulders back, relax, look straight ahead and when the judge addresses the court turn your attention to them. Do not, for any reason, during the game make a noise or try to communicate with them. Remain hemotionless, listen to every word that's spoken but do not react to a single one, not even with a raised eyebrow. By all means enjoy the front-row view, but you'll be ejected if you think you have any right to argue the ref's calls. Listen attentively and try to follow how the judge is interpreting your case, but wait until after the siren has sounded to ask your solicitor's opinion.

The big day is an important day, a sign you have reached the second half of this game, and let's hope the wind's behind you. Matters may not be resolved on the first day of the hearing, but don't fret, another date will be set. Hopefully, you will walk away more knowledgeable, having gained a better understanding of your odds and the score. With a bit of luck, your team made a good first impression and was more agreeable than not, especially with the judge. You may walk away with something or empty-handed, but the second half is only just beginning. At least you will be more aware that the court is a place that is just, fair — and always right. Most of all, your house should be in order and in due course your requests could be accommodated.

68 Abiding by the decision

Golden rule 1: 'You both think you're right.'

At the end of this game there will be a decision, whether it is one you have reached through agreement with Jane, one negotiated through a mediator or a ruling made by a judge. Eventually there will be a decision, and with that a set of orders that clearly spell out the who, how, where and why of caring for your kids. To trust that the legal process will simply deliver up your children is to court disappointment, for the courts have a duty to consider, which is not simply about meeting your requests. It may not be you who is unwilling to come to a care arrangement of one kind or another, but if you have made genuine efforts to do this your actions will be evident.

One matter your solicitor may have broached with you is the possibility that the court may not find in your favour. When a decision is handed down by the court, it will be accompanied by an explanation of the judgment. The big question now is how you are going to deal with the result — good, bad or indifferent. They say a fair decision is a good decision. Court isn't a game, though, and nor is it a place where winners and losers are created.

> "When a decision is handed down by the court, it will be accompanied by an explanation of the judgment. The big question now is how you are going to deal with the result — good, bad or indifferent."

How the end result makes you feel is completely up to you. How you act post decision, after the whistle has sounded, is also completely up to you. But eventually the war will end, and a decision will be made along with some orders. Most importantly it is up to you to act in accordance with these orders. Taking the law into your own hands, or dishing out your own version of rough justice, is not a good idea at all. If the decision is not as favourable as you had hoped, try your best to keep your hemotions under control. You may have asked the court to decide for you and Jane, and in reality, this is what they have done in creating orders for your children's care.

There have been a number of horror stories on the 6 o'clock news and in the papers of fathers who have taken it upon themselves to protest the decision of the courts. If you have ever craved celebrity status, this is most certainly not the way to go about it. You may have had to endure more than you ever imagined during this process, and the result may be disappointing to the point of being soul destroying. But think before you involve your children in your grief. Everyone is much better off if you keep it to yourself. Go and see your doctor or work through it with a professional. Whatever you choose to do, make sure you don't vent your frustration on your kids. It's not their fault.

Taking your disappointment out on your solicitor, a mediator, the judge or Jane is also the wrong thing to do. Though the decision may greatly affect and shape the rest of your life and your ability to be a father, it is completely unreasonable, unnecessary and wrong to take out your pain on anyone else. Your pain is yours, so be a man and own it. Don't broadcast it or blight someone else's life with your despair. After all, the professionals are just doing their jobs, and most likely doing their best, whether it looks that way or not. There will be others who share your disappointment at the result, but blaming them won't change the result.

"Children grow up to be adults, just like you did, and will form their own opinions of the world."

If you feel that the decision is going to push you over the edge, take a big step back and think for a second how your kids would cope with the knowledge that their dad was no longer around. Children grow up to be adults, just like you did, and will form their own opinions of the world. One day most likely they will have kids of their own, just as you did, and may even have to go through the same painful experiences. In fact, one day this horrible experience may be something you can use to help them deal with a similar ordeal. There is no fat lady at the end of this day and certainly no song to be sung.

Accepting and abiding by the decision may be difficult, but you must. You can be sure that nothing good will come of any effort to exert some rough justice of your own. Instead, just love your kids, from close by or from afar. Be there for them, whether or not you can be physically with them. That's what fathers are renowned for, and when the chips are down, or things become too hard for them, they will need you and seek you out. Don't go missing, don't just disappear, don't be fatalistic and don't do anything that is likely to end up on the 6 o'clock news.

69 The big question

Golden rule 1: 'You both think you're right.'

The most important question you can raise as a parent is, what's best for my kids? Although this might seem like a 'how long is a piece of string' kind of question, it's the one a judge will be asking as they peruse your application for care. What you think as a father is important, and if Jane won't consider your views then a mediator or a court will. What matters is you have a clear and considered plan, which features your kids' interests above all, including your own.

Without knowing the answer to the big question, what will you be asking for? Knowing the answer will help you construct a plan that is practical, workable and sustainable. Coming up with a complicated solution based on fuzzy logic will bring you undone, so use the KISS formula and keep it simple, stupid. Kids thrive on continuity in their lives and so will you. Keeping your plan simple and regular is very different from seeking 'equality'. Confusing issues is the quickest way to mess up any plan, and employing hemotions won't help you formulate an answer either. Although many parenting plans work off a fortnightly calendar, if you can construct a plan that works week in week out, it will be easier for you to maintain and for Jane and your kids to understand. Ultimately, the simpler you can make it, the less that can go wrong and the better it will be for all involved. What is practical for you and the kids will also need to be simple enough for Jane to follow. You can save a lot of grief and heartache by reducing the chances of her claiming she got confused over what week it was or thought you were picking them up.

"The most important question you can raise as a parent is, what's best for my kids? "

Knowing what Jane will be able to do is an advantage, but coming up with a plan that you know she will fail to honour is not going to work in the long run. If Jane is seriously one of the country's worst drivers, remove any risk and do the driving yourself. It may not seem fair but at least you can reduce the risk of her failing to drop off the kids. Doing the driving is also a godsend if you like making plans, as you won't find yourself pacing around the house or listening to her excuses or traffic reports.

The more practical you make your plans, the easier they will be for Jane to maintain, and the easier it will be on you and your kids. The more workable your plans, the more you will be able to achieve. It's not about creating endless options for Jane but rather a plan that you honestly believe is fair and reasonable. Splitting the minutes of the week is not the way to work out a shared care agreement, trying to make your plans easy to agree with and work is. If you are able to pick the kids up from school or childcare, suggest it. Australian blokes have never been scared of a little work; the more willing you are to share the parenting workload, the better your outcome will be.

Your plan needs to show your willingness to contribute to the day-to-day maintenance of your children's lives, which goes well beyond making regular child support payments. The longevity of your plans is also important and will make them far more attractive to a mediator or a judge. Having plans that are sustainable is critical for all involved. Situations do change, more often than not for the good. People grow, and so do their likes and dislikes. Your kids will become teenagers and the success of your plan depends on a mature approach to accommodating such natural changes. It's not so much about having strategies for 'what if' as it is about making plans from what you already know and can contribute.

> "The one thing that won't change in your kids' lives is the fact that you're their father and Jane is their mother."

Foreseeable futures are just that, but no one really has the ability to predict them. The one thing that won't change in your kids' lives is the fact that you're their father and Jane is their mother. But what kind of a dad you'll be will depend on how well you plan for dealing with the changes life creates. Deciding what's best for your kids is a parent's right, but you need to be able to provide care to exercise this. If the task of developing a plan sounds a little daunting, don't panic. There are people who are skilled in designing them. But you will need to contribute and at least have a basic idea of what you think will work. You also need to be prepared to consider Jane's suggestions. The simpler the plan is, the greater its chances of success of providing a parental balance in your children's lives.

Sticking to these plans may restrict your spontaneous self, but hopefully they will run like clockwork and make the future far more predictable. And to go into mediation or sit in front of your solicitor with an admission that you haven't given it much thought is a bad idea and likely to end up costing you more in the long run. It may also result in you having to accept what Jane wants, and that may not be what you think is best for your kids.

70 The cost of it all

Golden rule 1: 'You both think you're right.'

You may as well put away the calculator because trying to count the cost of it all is near impossible. Sure, it's not hard to add up the legal bills, court costs and parking. But trying to quantify the value of people's support will make you realise that you're in some serious personal debt. Needless to say, a fair amount of sincere gratitude will go a long way when thanking those who rode with you on this one. The ride will have cost them too, so don't be surprised when they begin to ask favours of you in the years to come. If only we could answer the question 'Was this really necessary?' *before* embarking on this voyage. Hindsight may be a wonderful reflective tool, but it doesn't change a single thing. How long it took to achieve some form of parenting order will serve as a reminder to never take this detour in life again if you can truly help it.

"Playing tit for tat with Jane only ends up costing everyone."

The toll of this process and all the stress it creates either is self-inflicted or has been inflicted by Jane. In either case it should have been unnecessary. Playing tit for tat with Jane only ends up costing everyone, whether in legal to-ing and fro-ing, or in the length of time it takes to record petty events since your separation. But the biggest cost is the one to your kids. The legal bill might run a close second, but how the kids fare in all of this is partially a result of your actions. Keeping it together is just the start of what you have to do to ensure the kids aren't short-changed. You can't control Jane's mind, but you can refrain from making her mad, as only you know how. Your children will never know what this ordeal has really cost you, and nor should they. But the sooner you are able to achieve an outcome, the sooner they will begin to regain some paternal balance in their lives.

The cost of this can be as all-consuming as the Blob, and like June 30 it can be very taxing. How much and how long is not entirely under your control, but your actions can either resolve or prolong this sorry affair. Apart from the debts and IOUs underwritten by your word, supporters can never really be thanked enough for simply listening to you and your plight. Or being subjected to Jane's and her family's behaviour. There's a cost, both financially and emotionally, that may never be repaid. It's hard to recover what has been lost.

The damage the separation has done to your kids and your relationship can heal, but rarely is it fairly compensated. Two wrongs don't make a right — they make two wrongs. In the end, who would ever have thought just how much learning to agree with Jane would cost? Fortunately the sooner you work this out, the earlier it will stop costing you, your kids, your family and your friends.

71 The reasons why?

Golden rule 1: 'You both think you're right.'

For some blokes it may be the last question you ask your solicitor as you exit the court through its big wooden doors. For others, it's a question they will ask themselves for years to come. The sole purpose of this book is to prevent this question from ever being asked again. If the three golden rules weren't clear enough, then hopefully the 50,000 words of reason that followed helped to paint an honest picture of this jungle. No doubt there will be many factors that inform and shape the court's judgment. Some will be of critical importance and some will simply add weight to and influence other considerations.

The reasons why, whether or not you agree with them, will be considered, but just what is considered is shaped in part by your behaviour, actions and submissions. Argument is your enemy because it is fuel on the fire that's raged between you and Jane. The faster this can be brought under control, and possibly extinguished, the greater your chances are of achieving and maintaining an equitable parenting order. Arguments with Jane in your former life cannot be undone or erased, and yes, she might be like an elephant in that respect, but we can forgive even if we never really forget.

"Understanding the reasons why, is not rocket science, nor is it some great mystery."

Understanding the reasons why, is not rocket science, nor is it some great mystery. The first of the two primary considerations of the court is to weigh up the benefit to your kids of maintaining meaningful relationships with both their parents. This is ideally represented by a shared care arrangement, or at least a parenting order that provides for one or other parent to spend meaningful and significant time with their children. The second primary consideration is often the first hurdle that needs to be overcome, when the court is asked to consider if there is a need to protect the children from harm, exposure to abuse, neglect or family violence. If arguments are a thing of the past, then demonstrating this to the court is a must if you are to regain any ground you have lost through an explosion of hemotions or violence. Addressing your behaviour by seeking professional help may not seem like a manly thing to do, but it may improve your behaviour, your case, your relationship with Jane and your chances of having a meaningful relationship with your kids in the future.

The time you invest in your children needs to account for more than just the idea of 'quality time'. It should consider a multitude of your children's needs — from their physical environment to their educational, social, physical and spiritual development. Again, your afterlife with Jane is essential to achieving this, and maintaining a care agreement for your kids into the future. If the courts are needed to sort this out, the time you are willing and able to contribute to the regular care of your kids might be considered as significant. What you're prepared to do as the father of your children is all about what you'll be doing with the time you have with them and what you feel is best for them. There are all types of experiences to share with your children, though sharing the care of them will require you to understand there are some things that are simply not negotiable.

The type of home you are able to provide for your children, if a property settlement and family assets are involved, may ultimately be determined by the court, if they are left to settle the argument. There will be a direct relationship between how these assets are distributed and your ability to provide a suitable environment for your children. This determination will be based on the nature, length, contributions and benefits of your marriage or partnership in relation to each party. Sadly, the future earning potential of each parent, and not their financial contributions to the family, play a large part in determining how the assets are to be divided. There are, of course, other major factors that will determine the likelihood that your new home can accommodate your children, including for a start its proximity to Jane's. Your new living arrangements, if they are shared with family, mates or a new flame, could either be of immense benefit to you and your kids or a very real handicap in the eyes of a mediator or a judge. It's not the sacrifices you are prepared to make for your children that are likely to impress, but rather your effort to create an environment that is considered practical, safe, secure and beneficial to your children.

"Parenting isn't rocket science. It's a *social* science."

Parenting isn't rocket science. It's a *social* science. It's an environmental, economic, social, educational and spiritual responsibility. It's also probably the most personal human behaviour an adult ever exhibits. There's little comfort in realising most partnerships are not everlasting, and who's around to say that they ever were? Marriage vows and pledges are made from the heart, but are contractual and legally binding by their very nature. To avoid asking your counsel for the reasons why (although a judge may provide reasons for their decisions), practise the art of agreement rather than argument. It might sound simple but it is fundamental to resolving this situation for you, your kids, your family, your finances and what's left of your sanity. This opportunity is always available, throughout the entire process, in a variety of colours, shapes and sizes. All you need to do is put down your sword, control your hemotions and man-feelings, think about what you as a father have to offer, and seek a way to agree on what's best for your kids. Because — *warning, warning* — if you don't, you'll most certainly run the risk of ending up asking for the reasons why.

72 No regrets

Golden rule 1: 'You both think you're right.'

To emerge from the darkness of the jungle empty-handed would be disastrous. On the other hand, the one thing you do not want to emerge with is regret. A barrister, standing in the light of an aftermath, once said, 'Have no regrets'. This advice is philosophical but in reality is quite haunting and somewhat profound. You see, any regret over something that has or has not happened won't immediately come to hand, and it won't help to deploy a spacecraft to search the deep space of your mind. Regret is an agent of afterthought: it appears of its own accord, especially when you are least expecting it.

So, what is there to regret in all that you have been through? Some may regret the day they ever laid eyes on Jane. Others might regret not joining the French Foreign Legion when they had the chance. Perhaps it's impossible not to regret some things along this not-so-merry way. It may be you acted irrationally, or not soon enough, or your regret may come from something you're reluctant to talk about and aren't really proud of. So where are these regrets to be found? Are they things you wish had never happened or you could have done better? The answer, like the truth, is simple. If you're asking the question, they obviously haven't arrived yet and most likely won't for some time. Because regret is something that happens in hindsight — not at the start, in the middle or at the end, but *after* an event, at a time that's yet to come.

> "Others might regret not joining the French Foreign Legion when they had the chance."

Which regret will be first to arrive or the worst is purely academic. As humans we cannot change the past, and this is where our regrets come from. There is no point blaming oneself for doing something wrong. Often regret is only realised when there is a consequence attached. It's not till the dust has settled that you may start seeing the errors of your ways, and realise that fighting is only destructive. Of course, life is about learning, though this is one of the hardest lessons a father can be taught.

The one thing all fathers should be sure of is they have no regrets about having children. Whether or not they are planned, children bring great joy to any father's life. Our kids are how we live on in nature, and let's face it, you would not have taken up this challenge if you didn't love your kids. To regret love is to regret life, and to regret your children, put simply, would be an extremely bloody selfish thing to do. It might be possible to emerge from the jungle with no regrets, but to achieve this you will need to have stayed on track, played by the rules, listened to advice and found a path to agreement. Saving your hemotions for the kids, rather than allowing them to govern your actions, might have saved you much time, money and heartache. But most important of all, knowing you can achieve a good result for your kids through a resolution of one sort or another may prove the most satisfying flavour, one that can wash away all taste of regret.

AFTER

EVERY

ENDING

IS

A

NEW

BEGINNING

www.ingramcontent.com/pod-product-compliance
Lightning Source LLC
LaVergne TN
LVHW100325210926
848480LV00003B/1260
9780992406509